QuiltPink

for hope

Meredith® Books
Des Moines, Iowa

QuiltPink *for hope*

Contributing Editor: Carol Field Dahlstrom
Contributing Graphic Designer: Angie Haupert Hoogensen
Associate Design Director: Som Inthalangsy
Copy Chief: Terri Fredrickson
Copy Editor: Kevin Cox
Publishing Operations Manager: Karen Schirm
Senior Editor, Asset and Information Management: Phillip Morgan
Edit and Design Production Coordinator: Mary Lee Gavin
Art and Editorial Sourcing Coordinator: Kathy Stevens
Editorial Assistant: Kaye Chabot
Book Production Managers: Pam Kvitne, Marjorie J. Schenkelberg,
 Mark Weaver
Imaging Center Operator: Kristin Reese
Contributing Copy Editor: Margaret Smith
Contributing Proofreaders: Julie Cahalan, Barb Rothfus,
 Mary Helen Schiltz
Contributing Technical Illustrator: Chris Neubauer

Meredith® Books
Editor in Chief: Gregory H. Kayko
Executive Director, Design: Matt Strelecki
Managing Editor: Amy Tincher-Durik
Executive Editor: Jennifer Darling
Senior Editor/Group Manager: Vicki Leigh Ingham
Senior Associate Design Director: Ken Carlson
Marketing Product Manager: Toye G. Cody

Executive Director, Marketing and New Business: Kevin Kacere
Director, Marketing and Publicity: Amy Nichols
Executive Director, Sales: Ken Zagor
Director, Operations: George A. Susral
Director, Production: Douglas M. Johnston
Business Director: Jim Leonard

Vice President and General Manager: Douglas J. Guendel

***Better Homes and Gardens*® Magazine**
Editor in Chief: Gayle Goodson Butler

Creative Collection
Editor in Chief: Deborah Gore Ohrn

Meredith Publishing Group
President: Jack Griffin
Senior Vice President: Karla Jeffries

Meredith Corporation
Chairman of the Board: William T. Kerr
President and Chief Executive Officer: Stephen M. Lacy

In Memoriam: E.T. Meredith III (1933–2003)

All of us at Meredith® Books are dedicated to providing you with
information and ideas to create beautiful and useful projects.
We welcome your comments and suggestions. Write to us at:
Meredith Books, Crafts Editorial Department, 1716 Locust Street—
LN126, Des Moines, IA 50309-3023.

Generous.

That's the first word that comes to mind when we think of quiltmakers. The readers of *American Patchwork & Quilting®* magazine have repeatedly proven that to be true. Our first fundraising event, Quilt for the Cure, brought in nearly 25,000 quilt blocks, which were made into quilts and auctioned on eBay, raising $100,000 for breast cancer research. When we announced our plans for Quilt Pink™ a year later, the response from quiltmakers and shop owners was overwhelming.

More than 1,100 quilt shops and guilds around the world—from all 50 states and nine countries—signed up to host a Quilt Pink event. On Quilt Pink Day (September 30, 2006), we estimate more than 100,000 quilters spent the day cutting, piecing, and quilting the nearly 4,000 quilts that were sent to us the following spring. We then auctioned those quilted treasures on eBay and as this book went to press, we were on track to contribute $200,000 to Susan G. Komen for the Cure, benefiting breast cancer research.

As you might imagine, that many quilts offered a wealth of inspiration, from one-of-a-kind art pieces to creative combinations of favorite patterns. Many quilts also came with stories. To celebrate the creativity and share the stories, we chose nearly 100 quilts to present in *Quilt Pink for Hope*. In keeping with the intent of the Quilt Pink events, we are pleased to contribute a portion of the proceeds from the sales of this book to Susan G. Komen for the Cure.

To participate in future Quilt Pink events, visit AllPeopleQuilt.com to find shops in your area that are signed up. Then contact the shop to see how you can get involved. Together, quilters can make a difference in the fight against breast cancer.

Happy Quilting,

The Editors, *American Patchwork & Quilting®* magazine

contents

inspiring quilt designs page 6

*Browse through a sampling of the exquisite quilts submitted for
Quilt Pink™ to be auctioned for breast cancer research. Then read
the heartwarming and inspiring stories told by their makers.*

quilt block patterns page 92

See patterns up close with complete instructions for making 50 quilt blocks.

Inspiring Quilt Designs

The quilts in this unique gallery are all beautifully different—yet all the same. They were stitched by quilters who gave their time and talent for the cause of finding a cure for breast cancer. Look at their works of art, read their stories, and feel the passion these quilters share.

Look closely and you will see words of encouragement and the names of women with breast cancer that Kathy Veltkamp quilted into this beautiful quilt.

Every quilt has a story

Kathy made this quilt to commemorate her dear friend, Julie Reed, a devoted wife and mother, who lost her battle with the disease. After her death, Julie's husband took her unused fabric to Kathy at Thimble Town, a quilt shop in Visalia, California. Kathy used the pink fabric to make this stunning quilt— a tribute to her dear friend and a very special woman.

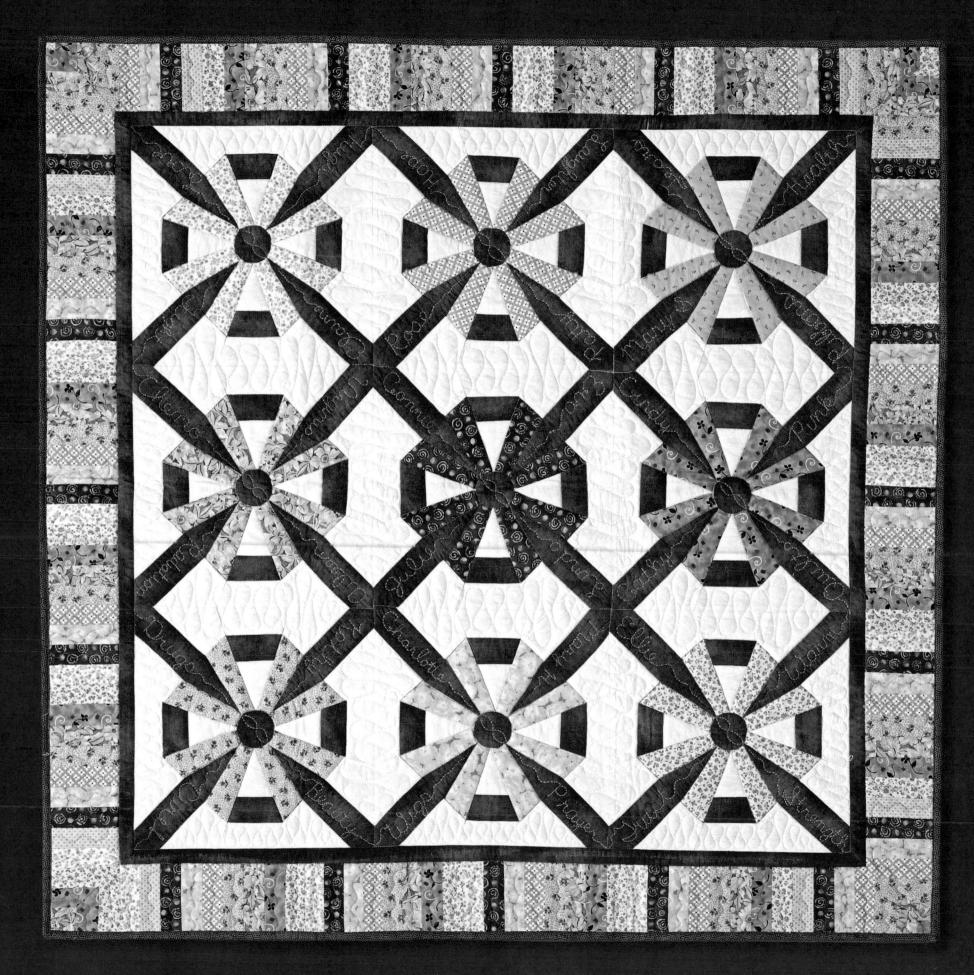

Ribbons from Julie's Pinks ◇ *Submitted by Thimble Town* ◇ *Visalia, California*

Debbie Richards of Quilter's Haven wanted to make a happy and beautiful quilt for all of the survivors of breast cancer. Mary Morris appliquéd the beautiful and intricate center block, and people received kits to create the posy blocks before Debbie finally assembled it.

She says, "We just wanted to put a smile on the faces of breast cancer survivors when they saw this pink quilt."

Every quilt has a story

In the Pink Posies ◇ *Submitted by Quilter's Haven* ◇ *Olathe, Kansas*

The dream of partners Robin King and Diane McKoen was to have a quilt shop in rural Oregon. Tater Patch Quilts is that dream come true.

One of their best customers is Nellie Tackas who is 100 years young. She has helped with almost every fundraising event at the store, including the quilt shown here for Quilt Pink. She also has made hundreds of Log Cabin quilts for Operation Quilts to send to troops overseas.

Every quilt has a story

Boasting that this is the fourth war effort she has participated in, Nellie has also wrapped bandages, knitted socks, and sold war bonds. Her zest for life comes from her strong values, love of life and family, and sense of purpose and community—something that makes her a role model for everyone lucky enough to meet her.

Nellie's Quilt ◇ *Submitted by Tater Patch Quilts* ◇ *Merrill, Oregon*

This lovely quilt is a crazy Log Cabin pattern with roses in the centers. Christine Storm of Port Orford, Oregon, lovingly stitched it. Christine relates,

"My sister and I are both breast cancer survivors. When I heard that her daughter-in-law was going to have the first baby girl in the family, I gathered all my pink fabrics and made us each a pink ribbon quilt, hoping that the next generation will not have to worry about breast cancer. When I heard about the Quilt Pink project, I thought my quilt would do more good being auctioned off than just hanging on my quilt rack."

Every quilt has a story

Log Cabin Roses ⋄ *Submitted by Forget Me Knots* ⋄ *Bandon, Oregon*

*P*ink sampler quilt blocks were made by women all over Michigan and almost every block was made in honor of a breast cancer survivor.

Every quilt has a story

The blocks were displayed in the charming Hollyhock Quilt Shoppe owned by Dick and Denise Hartz of Harrisville, Michigan. Stories about how breast cancer affected these women were posted as well. Cindi Van Hurk, the manager of the shop says,

"The quilters who made the blocks represent stitchers of every age and skill level, with one thing in common—a desire to help fight the disease."

Pink Sherbet ◦ *Submitted by Hollyhock Quilt Shoppe* ◦ *Harrisville, Michigan*

*M*oonlighters, a division of the Pass Patchers in Beaumont, California, pieced this sweet heart quilt. The quilt represents many breast cancer victims and survivors. As the women came together they had a chance to share their stories.

Georgia, the shop owner, writes, "The Quilt Pink project was personally an eye-opener for me because I had no idea how many women that I know have had to fight this battle.

We appreciate the fun and memories that were made on this Quilt Pink Day."

Every quilt has a story

Enduring Hearts ◇ *Submitted by Georgia's Quilting Obsession* ◇ *Beaumont, California*

Connie Hefte made this quilt submitted by Hidden Quilts in Platteville, Wisconsin. The pattern she chose is called Amazing Grace, which she thought was appropriate for the cause.

Every quilt has a story

Connie says, "Because my mother-in-law and my next door neighbor each went through a breast removal this past year, I wanted to do something to help the cause. Both women are doing great, I'm happy to say."

Amazing Grace ◊ *Submitted by Hidden Quilts* ◊ *Platteville, Wisconsin* ◊ *Design by Handmaiden Designs*

The Friendship Star Quilters from the Long Island Quilters Society are a small group that meets several times a month.

They were inspired to create a quilt for Quilt Pink by two members, Cheryl Blam and Jane Rosen, who showed such courage in their battles with breast cancer. Storm at Sea showcases a traditional block, chosen to represent the "storm" that all those diagnosed with cancer go through.

The quilt is handpieced; it was quilted by Dot Seelig of Bayside, New York.

Every quilt has a story

Storm at Sea ◇ *Submitted by Long Island Quilters' Society* ◇ *Mineola, New York*

*P*atti Chartrand, president of
North Star Quilters, writes for her
small guild of 30 quilters.

"We made the quilt
blocks and then
put them together
as a group on Quilt
Pink Day.

Every quilt has a story

We chose the pattern Scrapaholic
by Trudie Hughes. We love to do
quilts for charity and were excited
to quilt for Quilt Pink."

Pink Scrapaholic ◇ *Submitted by North Star Quilters Guild* ◇ *Vancouver, Washington* ◇ *Design by Trudie Hughes*

Melani Moyle and Kathy David of Between Friends Quilting in Tomahawk, Wisconsin, held a contest to see who could make the loveliest quilt block for Quilt Pink. It was difficult to pick the best block, but the paper-pieced rose in the center of the quilt was a favorite.

Everyone who made a block got a pink pin, a pink prize, and a pattern. All the quilters dressed in pink, and pink refreshments were served. The blocks were assembled into quilts to be auctioned.

Melani and Kathy named the shop Between Friends not only because they are friends, but because they want everyone who comes in the shop to feel that they are among friends. No doubt they do.

Every quilt has a story

Between Friends ◇ *Submitted by Between Friends Quilting* ◇ *Tomahawk, Wisconsin*

Marlene Capehart pieced the Log Cabin quilt in honor of her cousin Carol Vida, a breast cancer survivor.

Every quilt has a story

She chose a Log Cabin pattern because the center of each block represents the hearth of the home. The dark and light symbolize good and bad things that happen to us in our lives:

The cabin in the center of the quilt represents home and family who gather to support those who are suffering and to celebrate life for the survivors.

Pink Log Cabin ◇ *Quilts by Eagle Mountain Products* ◇ *Azle, Texas*

Lisa Johnson and the women of The Picket Fence Quilt Company from Wichita, Kansas, took a traditional Nine-Patch quilt block and created this stunningly colorful tribute to Quilt Pink. Bright colors frame the simple Nine-Patch blocks. The quilting on the blocks is done with interlocking hearts and bows are quilted in the white setting squares. Words of hope are quilted on the edges of the quilt.

Every quilt has a story

Quilt of Words ◇ *Submitted by The Picket Fence Quilt Company* ◇ *Wichita, Kansas*

The Brewster Bag Ladies are a group of six quilters from Cape Cod, Massachusetts, who have been together for about 10 years.

Every quilt has a story

When the local quilt shop announced the Quilt Pink event, it seemed perfect for the group because they had recently lost one of their dearest members to breast cancer. Another member is a breast cancer survivor.

Considering that someone might spend time cuddled under the quilt, they decided to make the quilt visually interesting in both design and fabric with a dynamic design of star patterns in various sizes.

Stars in Pink ◇ *Submitted by Tumbleweed Quilt Shop* ◇ *West Barnstable, Massachusetts*

Rosemary Dettlaff, a six-year breast cancer survivor, and Carol Sharp, the coordinator of Quilt Pink Day at Ralph's Sewing & Vac, joined together to make this clever kitty quilt. Independently, Rosemary stitched the cats with the tails on the left and Carol sewed the cats in reverse, hoping not to duplicate any fabric.

They both love kitties and thought that this pink kitty quilt would make people smile, as well as raise money for the cause.

Every quilt has a story

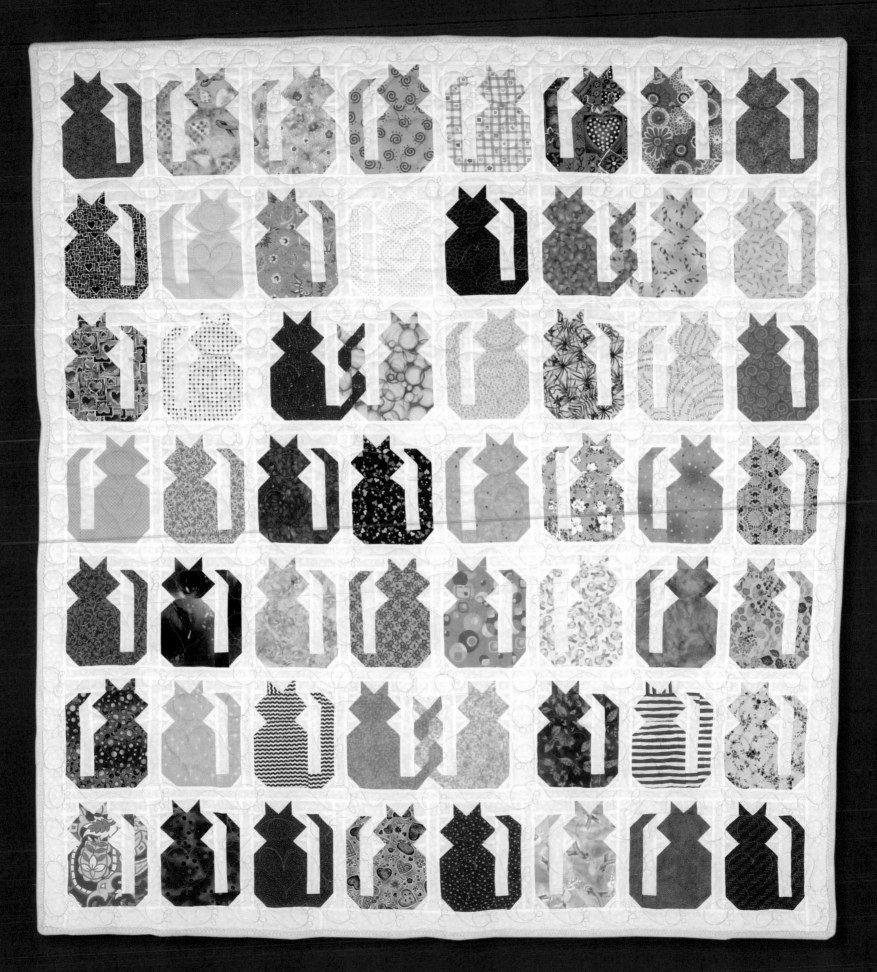

Rosemary's Kitties ◇ *Submitted by Ralph's Sewing & Vac* ◇ *Palm Desert, California*
Design by Jazz Cats from Janet Kime's The Cat's Meow: Purr-fect Quilts for Cat Lovers

Owner Rhonda McCann of
The Quilting Needle has used
quilting as a focus for women's
issues for years.

This quilt called Weaver Fever was a
collaborative effort by Rhonda and Amy Grott.

Every quilt has a story

Amy writes, "In many
situations breast cancer has
become a common thread
that binds women and men
together. It has touched my
life through several family
members and friends. I am
amazed by the strength and
courage of these individuals
and the message of hope."

Weaver Fever ⋄ *Submitted by The Quilting Needle* ⋄ *Trafford, Pennsylvannia* ⋄ *Quilt Design by Jacie Robinson*, Weaver Fever
Ribbon Border treatment by Eleanor Burns, Stars Across America

These handkerchief-style embroidered designs were created by Donna Morton especially for Quilt Pink. She was inspired by a simple heart shape—a symbol of love and remembrance. On Quilt Pink Day, Kathy Schroter, owner of Snip & Stitch Sewing Centre, reported a huge response to the event. "If people couldn't sew they brought food to share."

Note: Download embroidery heart patterns at www.snipandstitch.com.

Every quilt has a story

Embroidered Hearts ◇ *Submitted by Snip & Stitch Sewing Centre* ◇ *Nanaimo, British Columbia, Canada*

Taking inspiration from current color trends, the women in the Frisco Quilt Guild created this high-contrast quilt using instructions from *American Patchwork & Quilting* magazine.

Anne Bartholet of the Frisco Quilt Guild writes, "Breast cancer has touched most of our members in a personal way. We had our largest participation ever, with 97 blocks turned in."

Every quilt has a story

This guild has 91 members and focuses on service to others. In addition to Quilt Pink, they donated almost 200 quilts to family services, 100 quilts to veterans' hospitals and gave away more than 1000 Christmas stockings.

Bubble Gum and Chocolate ◇ *Submitted by Frisco Quilt Guild* ◇ *Frisco, Texas*

Gini Ewers wrote that Karil Walthers led a group of about a dozen women, each ready with an array of pink fabrics, in constructing the blocks for this quilt.

The variety of fabrics is as great as the variety of women, reflecting differences in age, style, and taste.

Gini says, "As I arranged my collections of blocks I was struck by how well the blocks worked together in spite of their incredible variety— how the placement of certain blocks next to each other seemed to enhance them both. We can do that for each other—as quilters, as women, as survivors, and as supporters."

Every quilt has a story

Ribbons of Hope ◇ *Submitted by Stitcher's Crossing* ◇ *Madison, Wisconsin*

ue Campbell of the Tumbleweed Quilt Shop on Cape Cod says that this layered and beaded design is actually easy to create.

On Cape Cod the beach rose (*Rosa rugosa*) is a perfect example of determination and resilience against the summer winds and winter storms. These beautiful wild flowers survive the elements by sinking their roots in sandy soil—they keep growing year after year.

Every quilt has a story

Sue and the women of this quilt shop found this flower and its survival, a fitting analogy to breast cancer survivors.

Rosa Rugosa ◇ *Submitted by Tumbleweed Quilt Shop* ◇ *West Barnstable, Massachusetts*

There are nearly 90 members in this active guild, and when *American Patchwork & Quilting* asked for finished quilts for Quilt Pink, this group went to work.

With no local quilt shop in the area, the Gone to Pieces Quilt Guild joined efforts at the Alpena Regional Medical Center Cancer Center. The women finished five quilts. One was raffled off at the hospital, raising $1,268 for the Cancer Center.

Pennie Morrison says, "We hope by helping that someday soon breast cancer can be at a minimum. We have many ladies and their family members who have been affected by the disease."

Every quilt has a story

Hearts Afire ◇ *Submitted by Gone to Pieces Quilt Guild* ◇ *Presque Isle, Michigan*

Calico Hutch in Hayward, Minnesota, offers a block-of-the-month program. When it was announced that this one was for Quilt Pink, 240 participants signed up—a remarkable number considering the population of Hayward is 230 people!

Using the block Crowned Cross, each member made blocks and several people assembled the quilt top.

Every quilt has a story

"The idea of having so many women working together to fight breast cancer was indeed exciting," writes Carolyn Matson, owner of Calico Hutch.

Crown and Cross ◇ *Submitted by Calico Hutch* ◇ *Hayward, Minnesota*

Kay Uhlenhaker and Jane Miller, both regular customers at the Richland Sewing Center in Hurst, Texas, combined their talents to create this quilt. Kay designed the top center square. In Kay's words,

"I wanted something circular. It stood for being surrounded by love, family, friends, talented doctors, and nurses. At the center of the block I embroidered scripture and a heart, which stood for my faith and the love of Christ for me. My faith in God has helped me through two different episodes of breast cancer. I pray that people will be blessed by this project.

Remember that you are loved by God and that He is always there to sustain you."

Every quilt has a story

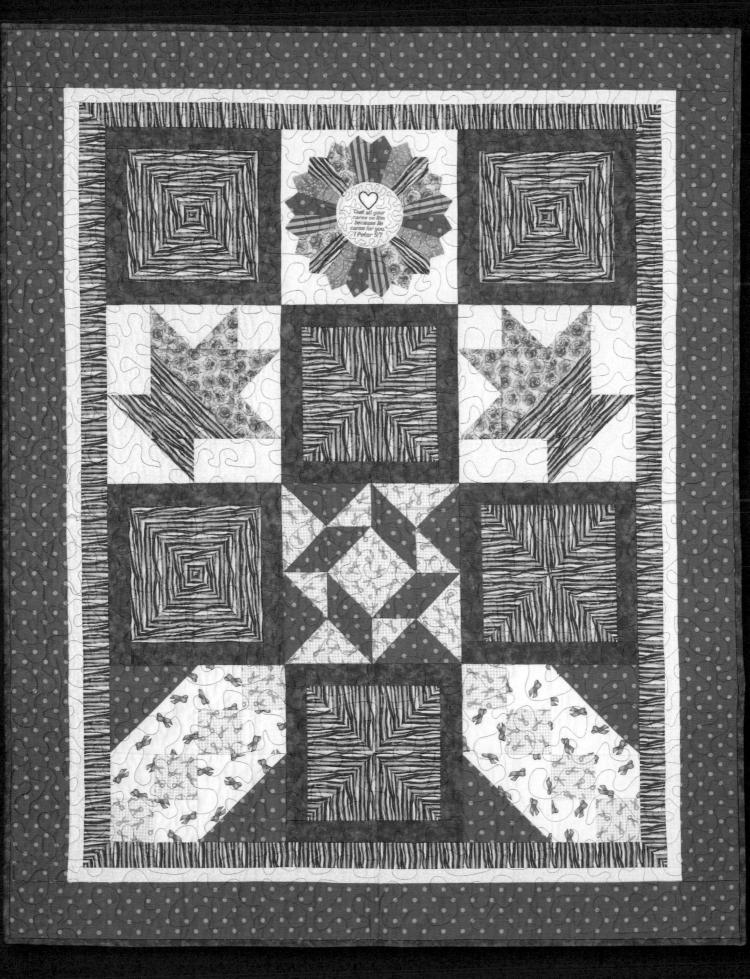

Pink Sampler ◇ *Submitted by Richland Sewing Center* ◇ *Hurst, Texas*

*L*aura Olsen writes that breast cancer has touched nearly everyone in their group. One member is a 30-year survivor; another member was diagnosed as the quilt was being made. An additional reason to make the quilt was to spend more time together–talking, eating, sewing, laughing, and enjoying life together.

Every quilt has a story

The women made new friends, strengthened the bonds between old friends, and realized that their group is a true survivor.

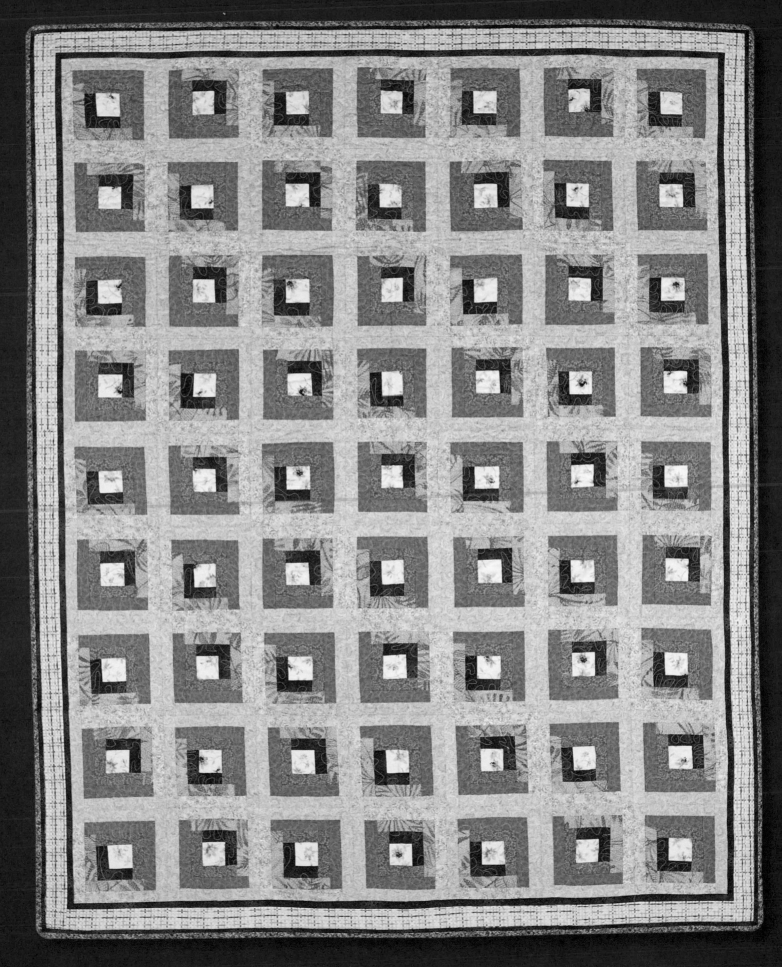

Pink Log Cabin Together ◇ *Submitted by Glad Creations Inc. Quilt Block* ◇ *Minneapolis, Minnesota*

Barbara Hildreth submitted this quilt to Grace Marko and Barbara Johnson at Tea & Textiles in Jefferson, Wisconsin. It was submitted along with 20 other quilts to *American Patchwork & Quilting* to be auctioned for the Quilt Pink event.

Barbara writes about her quilt, "I enjoy appliqué and embroidery. I saw the embroidery block in the quilt shop and was drawn to it. I made some changes and got started.

I made this quilt for my mom, great-aunt, and cousin—all of whom are breast cancer survivors. I also made it for my daughter, dad, and others in my family. With each stitch I took I thought of each person and what they had gone through and how much I loved and cared for each one. There are five blocks, one for each of the ladies, including my daughter."

Every quilt has a story

Ladies in Pink ◇ *Submitted by Tea & Textiles Quilt Shop* ◇ *Jefferson, Wisconsin*

After reading about Quilt Pink, Elaine Leko found some patterns originally designed for pillows that featured embroidered sentiments. She contacted the designer, Leslie Riley, to see whether she could use the designs. Leslie offered to make a Quilt Pink version of the designs if Elaine would find someone to put them into a quilt.

Shelly Koren and Bridget Westbrock joined the team. Bridget added a guardian angel motif when quilting this project.

Every quilt has a story

Elaine says, "We send this quilt with the prayer that it makes a difference, and that there is a goundbreaking discovery as we get closer to a cure for this dreaded disease."

Courage, Hope, Friendship ⋄ *Submitted by Silver Lane Quilting* ⋄ *New Brighton, Minnesota* ⋄ *Design by Leslie Riley,* The Primitive Heart

*L*ori Getz who lost both her mother and sister to breast cancer writes, "As women, we have all been touched by breast cancer. I am amazed how readily quilters will volunteer their time to make quilts to benefit whatever cause, but particularly the cancer that seems to target women."

At Lori's store the staff believes in the therapy of cloth and in the therapy of sisterhood. Lori continues, "We are touched by the stories of the ladies who come to our store—those without hair, wearing caps or scarves, and looking for the comfort of fabric and a friendly face.

Some of them have only a small amount of time left to complete a quilt that they will leave for a beloved— something that will prove that they really did exist."

Every quilt has a story

Remember Spring ◇ *Submitted by Quilter's Cupboard* ◇ *Atascadero, California* ◇ *Designed by Janet Nesbitt*

This Log Cabin quilt was pieced and quilted by the Mixed Sampler Quilt Guild of Siren, Wisconsin, with help from many neighbors and friends from surrounding communities in Minnesota and Wisconsin.

Every quilt has a story

Guild members donated 2-inch strips in various shades of dark and light pinks. Then the local quilt shop volunteered new sewing machines and additional fabric.

On Quilt Pink Day tables were covered with pink tablecloths for the refreshments, and everyone wore pink aprons. There were many laughs, stories, and memories shared as volunteers sewed blocks for the quilt.

Mixed Sampler Log Cabin ⋄ *Submitted by Mixed Sampler Quilt Guild* ⋄ *Siren, Wisconsin*

Quilters Unlimited Guild of northern Virginia was founded in 1972 with the purpose of preserving the tradition and culture of quilting. It has 12 chapters. The "Little Old Ladies" (as they call themselves) of the Mt. Vernon Chapter gathered together to create this sampler quilt, Twist and Turn for the Cure.

The members submitted a block of their choice and went to a full-day retreat. On the same day thousands of other quilters around the world were stitching for the cure as well, united by the Quilt Pink event.

Every quilt has a story

Twist and Turn for the Cure ⋄ *Submitted by Quilters Unlimited* ⋄ *Alexandria, Virginia*

Jean Roberts writes, "When I first heard about the Quilt Pink Day project, I knew that I wanted to be a part of it.

My sister and I were diagnosed with breast cancer within weeks of each other. I survived. Susie did not, leaving behind two young daughters. I also have two daughters."

Every quilt has a story

At Stitcher's Crossing's annual retreat, Jean asked if anyone would help with the Quilt Pink project. Everyone said yes. Jean supplied the background pink-ribbon fabric and the other quilters used their choice of pink fabrics to make the blocks using the Starflower pattern.

Starflower ⋄ *Submitted by Stitchers Crossing* ⋄ *Madsion, Wisconsin*

Sixteen women participated in this lovely quilt's creation—six of them were breast cancer survivors. Susan Wesner of Baron's Fabrics writes,

"We knew of their journey through treatment and witnessed the dignity and grace they displayed as they fought the good fight."

This three-fabric quilt showcases fabric designed by Luana Rubin for Robert Kaufman Fabrics. This designer, too, has been touched by the disease with the loss of her young daughter to cancer. Proceeds from the sale of this fabric are dedicated to cancer research.

Every quilt has a story

Joie-de-Vivre ⋄ *Submitted by Baron's Fabrics* ⋄ *Camarillo, California* ⋄ *Puzzle Box, Designed by Tracy Brookshier*

Quilter's Quarter is located in a small town in South Dakota in a restored Queen Anne building that is on the National Register of Historic Places. Quilt Pink became the theme for a popular event that Quilter's Quarter has every year.

Every quilt has a story

Susan Southrada shares, "A friend of mine was diagnosed with breast cancer as we were beginning our event. I cannot tell you what it meant making this quilt while Barb was struggling with the disease.

Not only could I give her flowers after her surgery, but I was fighting the battle with her by helping the Quilt Pink project—donating the quilt and collecting donations and raising women's awareness about the disease."

Pink Bows and More ⬦ *Submitted by Quilter's Quarter* ⬦ *Tabor, South Dakota*

This cheerful quilt was made by Girl Scout Troop No. 876 from Alden, New York, as part of the Silver Award Project—the highest award that a Cadette Girl Scout can earn. The scouts chose Breast Cancer Awareness as their topic. Girls ages 11 to 14, designed the quilt and chose the material to be used. Each girl sewed a heart square using paper piecing. The girls also chose a topic relating to breast cancer, researched the topic, and made a poster to display in the community. It is the hope of this Cadette Troop to raise awareness and educate the community about breast cancer and to show support for all women who experience this disease.

Every quilt has a story

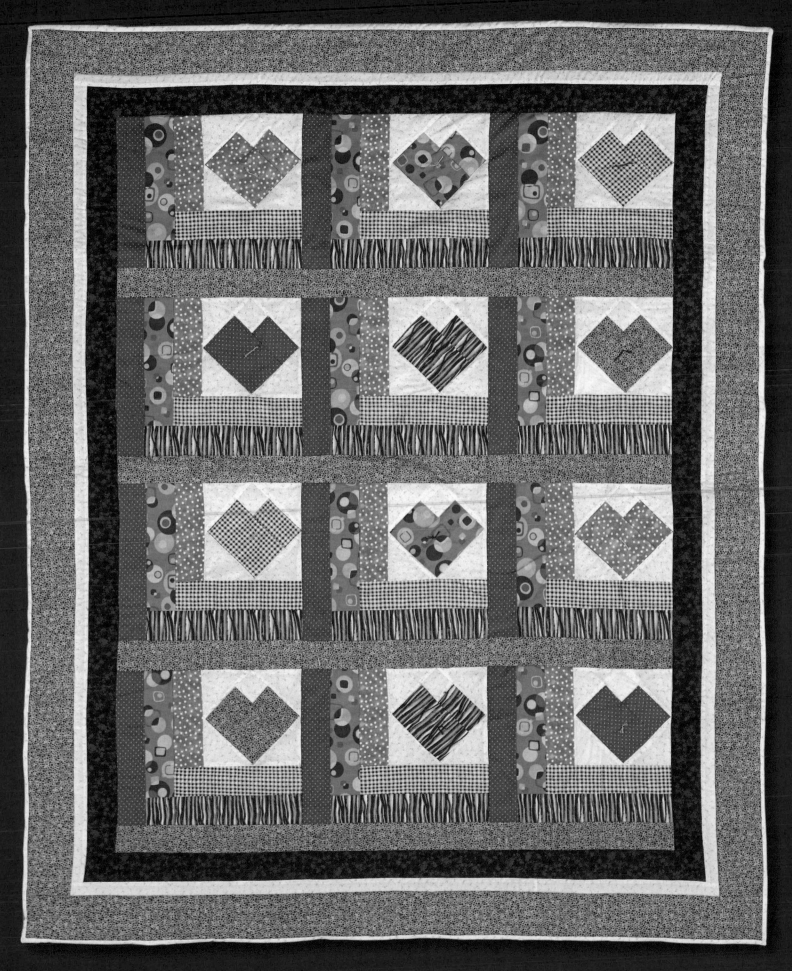

Pretty and Pink ◇ *Submitted by Girl Scout Troup No. 876* ◇ *Alden, New York*

_M_rs. Juliane Boehm's third- and fourth-grade classes in Jenera, Ohio, pieced together this _Ribbons of Prayers_ quilt. The top was designed by Ruth Grihalva. She and her husband, Rick, own Forever in Stitches in Bluffton, Ohio.

Each student sewed two blocks, and the quilt was assembled by Ruth with assistance from mothers, grandmothers, and other ladies from Trinity Evangelical Lutheran Church. Rick notes that the children learned so much.

Every quilt has a story

One little one said, "It helped our teacher and me. Mrs. Boehm's friend has cancer, and I thought of Grandma who died with it." Another exclaims, "The sewing machines made the music as we made the quilt blocks!"

Ribbons of Prayers ⋄ *Submitted by Forever in Stitches, LLC* ⋄ *Bluffton, Ohio*

The blocks for this quilt, tied with tiny fabric bows, were made by Cobblestone Quilters of Raymond, Maine. Many of the members of this group experienced the effects of breast cancer either personally or through family members and friends.

On the back of the quilt, written in pink, are names of members, sisters, mothers, daughters, grandmothers, granddaughters, aunts, nieces, and friends who have had breast cancer.

Carol McLeod writes, "Although this quilt was not dedicated to one person, each of us thought of how this disease has affected those we love. The Cobblestone group felt that making a quilt together would help us support each other, remember those who have passed, and benefit research."

Every quilt has a story

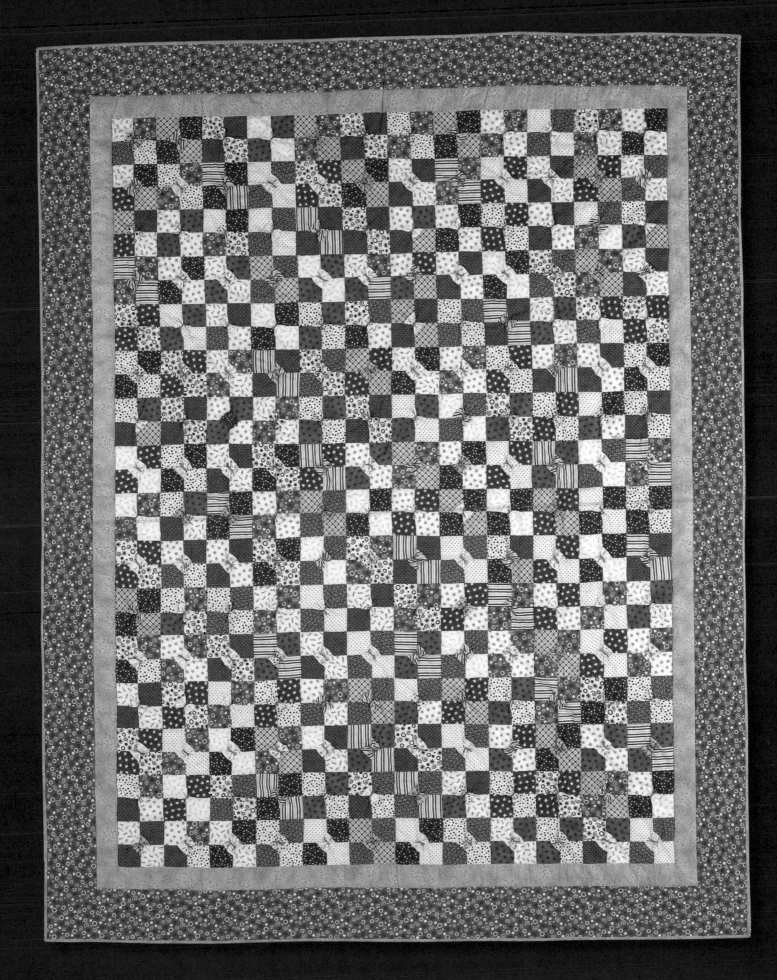

Bows of Comfort ◇ *Submitted by Cobblestone Quilters* ◇ *Raymond, Maine*

More than 40 volunteers met to sew this Delectable Mountains quilt in the shop owned by Peggy Jo Patterson at Peggy's Sewing Center. Peggy's mother was planning to do the quilting, but shortly after the top was pieced, Peggy's father became ill and her mother needed to change her plans.

"So while I was at my parents house in Salisbury, Maryland, my grandmother, age 94, decided to do the quilting. My grandmother helped me pin the quilt on the rack and she picked out the thread color as I chose the quilting design.

Every quilt has a story

Quilting helped to distract me from the emotions surrounding my dad's death. He died shortly after we quilted Delectable Mountains. I think about the hills and valleys in life every time I see this quilt."

Delectable Mountains ◇ *Submitted by Peggy's Sewing Center* ◇ *Centreville, Maryland*

This quilt entitled Hearts Blooming for the Cure came from a small group of quilters who had just learned to paper-piece. They decided to use their new skills to contribute to Quilt Pink. The quilt was professionally quilted by Angela McClelland, who also stitched the outline of a bumble bee into one corner of the white top to symbolize the name of the group— Bee Inclined. Maggie Davis writes, "We enjoyed the opportunity to come together as a group, to learn new techniques, and to produce an object that adds real value to the cause."

Every quilt has a story

Hearts Blooming for the Cure ◇ *Submitted by Bee Inclined Mini Group* ◇ *Incline Village, Nevada*

The Brubaker Sewing Center in the heart of Amish Country often participates in quilt shows. This quilt was made for the Quilt Odyssey Show in Hershey, Pennsylvania. Kits were distributed to make the blocks.

Every quilt has a story

Each kit of fabric included a Hershey's Kiss wrapped in a square of pink tulle with a thank you card attached. It let each quilter know her efforts would go towards finding a cure for breast cancer.

Amy Smith writes, "As a seven-year survivor I was thrilled to have the opportunity to participate in this wonderful event. The quilt, not dedicated to anyone in particular, is made to represent all the women who have the love and courage to battle the disease."

Hershey Kiss Quilt ◇ *Submitted by Brubaker Sewing Center* ◇ *New Holland, Pennsylvania*

This quilt was a community effort. The owners of Roelof's Store in Sioux Center, Iowa, made up kits of fabric and patterns for 6-inch blocks. The kits were distributed to 27 volunteers from the area, who stitched the blocks.

A store employee who has two sisters with the disease designed the quilt, determining how to arrange the blocks. Another employee sewed the rows together.

The women from the store write, "We all look forward to the day when a cure will be found and hope that money raised from this project will hasten the day that it will happen."

Every quilt has a story

Friendship Stars and Checks ⋄ *Submitted by Roelof's Store* ⋄ *Sioux Center, Iowa*

This modified Log Cabin quilt, made by Paula Ellison Christopherson, is in memory of her grandmother, Evelyn Anderson Smith.

Every quilt has a story

Paula writes, "Grandmother lived through the Depression and supported her family by working as a housekeeper in Great Falls, Montana. It wasn't until after World War II that Grandmother Evelyn was able to buy anything for herself. I remember vividly that her wardrobe contained joyful florals, bright colors, and fanciful costume jewelry. In 1953, she was diagnosed with breast cancer and fought the disease until her death in 1975. I know I inherited my love of fabrics from her. She faced many hardships in her life with courage and determination. I am fortunate to have the opportunity to honor her memory with this quilt."

One Heart ◇ *Submitted by Silver Lane Quilting Inc.* ◇ *New Brighton, Minnesota*

This Jacob's Ladder variation was designed by Linda Welch and pieced and quilted by Lois Southard and Teri Sartain.

Linda writes, "I designed the pattern that we used in the shop for Quilt Pink Day.

The pattern came from an idea I had to make blocks that would be connected to each other—like our lives are connected to each other through quilting."

Every quilt has a story

Connected ◇ *Submitted by Cabin Fever Quilt Shoppe* ◇ *Auburn, California*

Pam Tuttle at Bayside Quilting writes, "This quilt uses an original pattern designed by Martha Liska. Martha is of Czech heritage. I lived in the country for some time so we have a Bohemian bond—and the quilt design seems Bohemian to me, so the name fits."

Every quilt has a story

Rosie the Riveter, a classic image from the World War II era, is a frequent motif for this group so she seemed a perfect choice to lead the fight with the slogan, "We can do it!"

At Quilt Pink Day everyone received a free pink Rosie T-shirt. The group made quilts for Quilt Pink and lap quilts for the oncologists' offices.

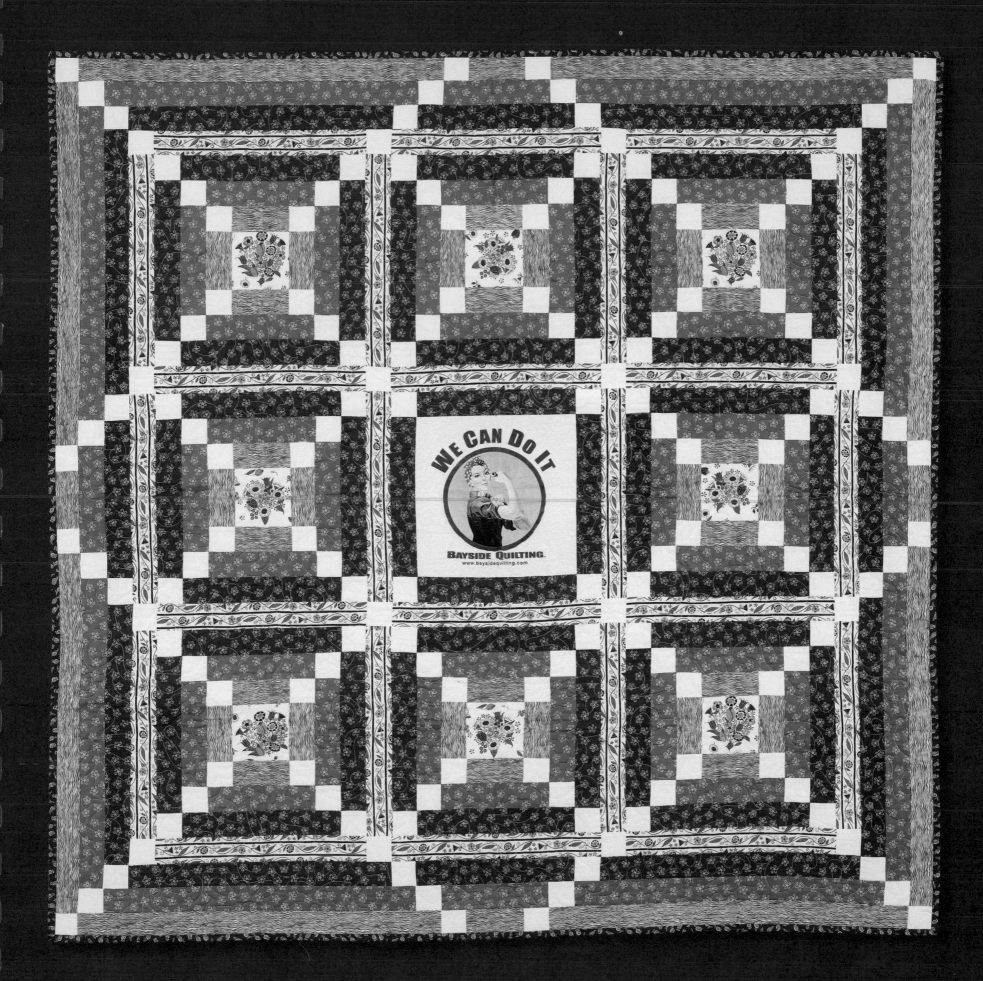

Rosie's Bohemian Chain ⋄ *Submitted by Bayside Quilting* ⋄ *Olympia, Washington*

Each person wants to help the cause in her own way. When the Glad Creations Quilt Block from Bloomington, Minnesota, advertised about Quilt Pink, they received all kinds of responses.

But they didn't expect that someone would drop off a quilt anonymously. Stitching on the beautiful quilt spells out words such as Mother, Mom, and Daughter.

One thing to be sure— the shapes on the quilt only reflect the big heart of someone who truly cares.

Every quilt has a story

Big Heart ⋄ *Submitted by Glad Creations Quilt Block* ⋄ *Bloomington, Minnesota*

Quilt Block Patterns

Choose from an array of quilt block patterns that appeared in some of the quilts submitted for the Quilt Pink auction. Although the blocks and quilts that were offered were a variety of sizes, the patterns shown are all 9-inch blocks for consistency. You'll also find alternate ways to assemble the blocks. To see the original quilts turn to page 194.

pieced butterfly

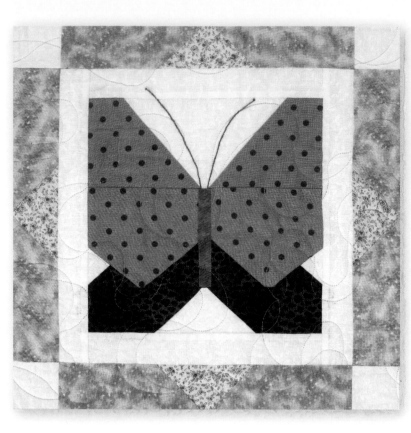

Rhonda Adams of Quilters Unlimited designed this butterfly block in honor of her mother, Elizabeth Adams, an 18-year breast cancer survivor. Rhonda says, "She is my friend, my mentor, and my inspiration." To see the entire quilt, turn to page 194.

Submitted by Quilters Unlimited
Mt. Vernon Chapter, Alexandria, Virginia

assemble the block

1 Make BCBr unit (4 times).
2 Add A to BCBr unit (2 times).
3 Make FGFr unit.
4 Make JKHL lower body unit.
5 Make LrHrKrJr lower body unit.
6 Sew I to center of lower body units.
7 Make MNMr unit. Sew 3 butterfly units together.
8 Sew D to top and bottom of unit.
9 Sew E to sides of unit.
10 Sew BcBr units to sides of E.
11 Sew ABCBr unit to top and bottom.
12 Embroider antennae using stem stitch.

try this

Make each butterfly in a different pastel color palette. A simple sashing with the same size corner squares used in the block completes the sweet yet elegant look.

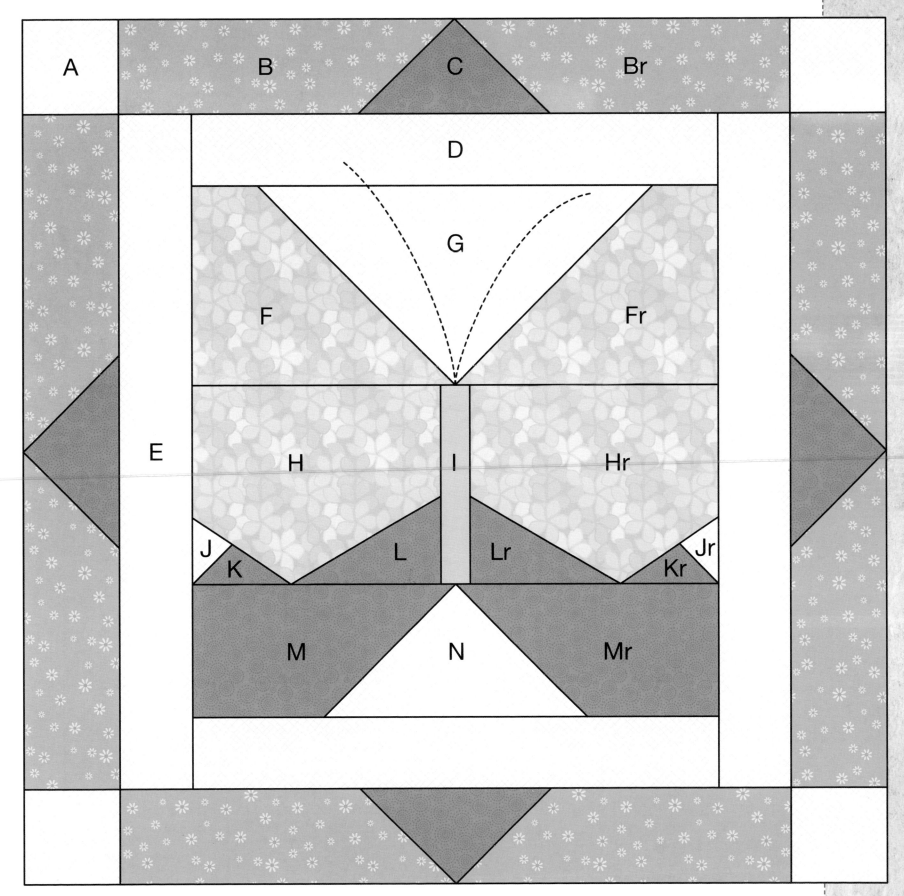

pieced butterfly full-size pattern

striped square

Women gathered in this small Minnesota town to create blocks and a striking quilt for the cause. To see the entire quilt, turn to page 194.

Submitted by Hingeley Road Quilt Shop
Floodwood, Minnesota

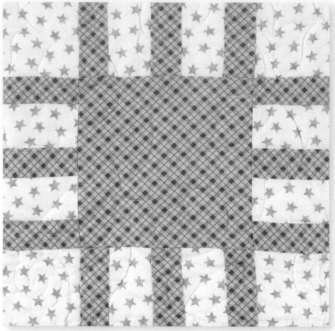

assemble the block

1 Make BBBBB unit (4 times).
2 Sew A to each end of BBBBB units (2 times).
3 Sew BBBBB vertically to opposite sides of C.
4 Sew rows together.

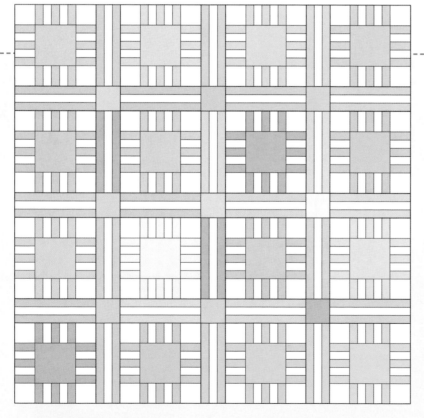

try this

Adding striped sashing in the same proportions as the blocks gives a strong geometric look.

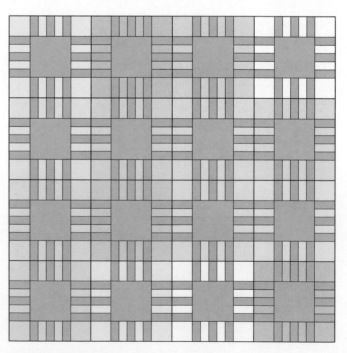

look again

Placing blocks side by side connects the stripes forming a larger block effect.

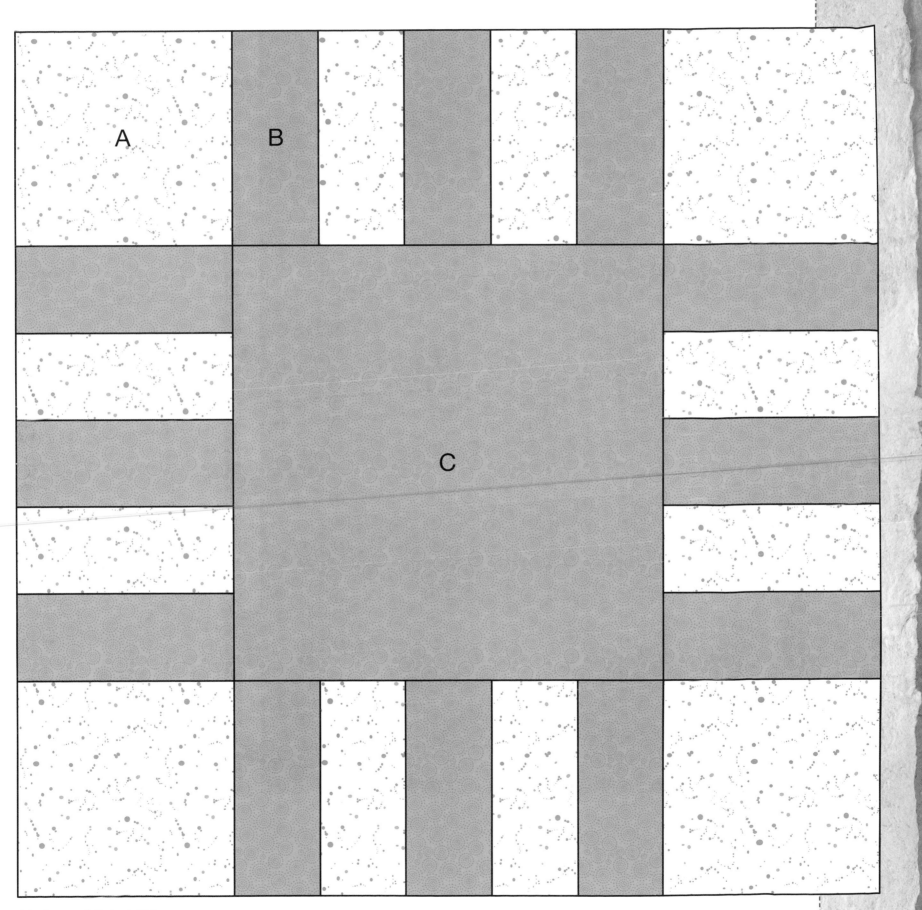

striped square full-size pattern

colorado block

Debra and Sandi became friends when Sandi came to Oak Harbor to undergo cancer treatments. They created this quilt together. Sandi is doing well and has since moved to be closer to her grandchildren. To see the entire quilt, turn to page 195.

Submitted by Quilters Workshop
Oak Harbor, Washington

assemble the block

1 Sew light A to dark A (8 times).
2 Sew dark A to each short side of B (4 times).
3 Join 4 AA units for center.
4 Sew AA to ABA and AA (2 times) to make Rows 1 and 3.
5 Sew ABA to opposite sides of center block to make Row 2.
6 Sew Row 1 to Row 2.
7 Add Row 3.

try this

With lights and darks placed as shown and positioned side by side, the blocks and pieced sashing create vertical and horizontal stripes of diamonds .

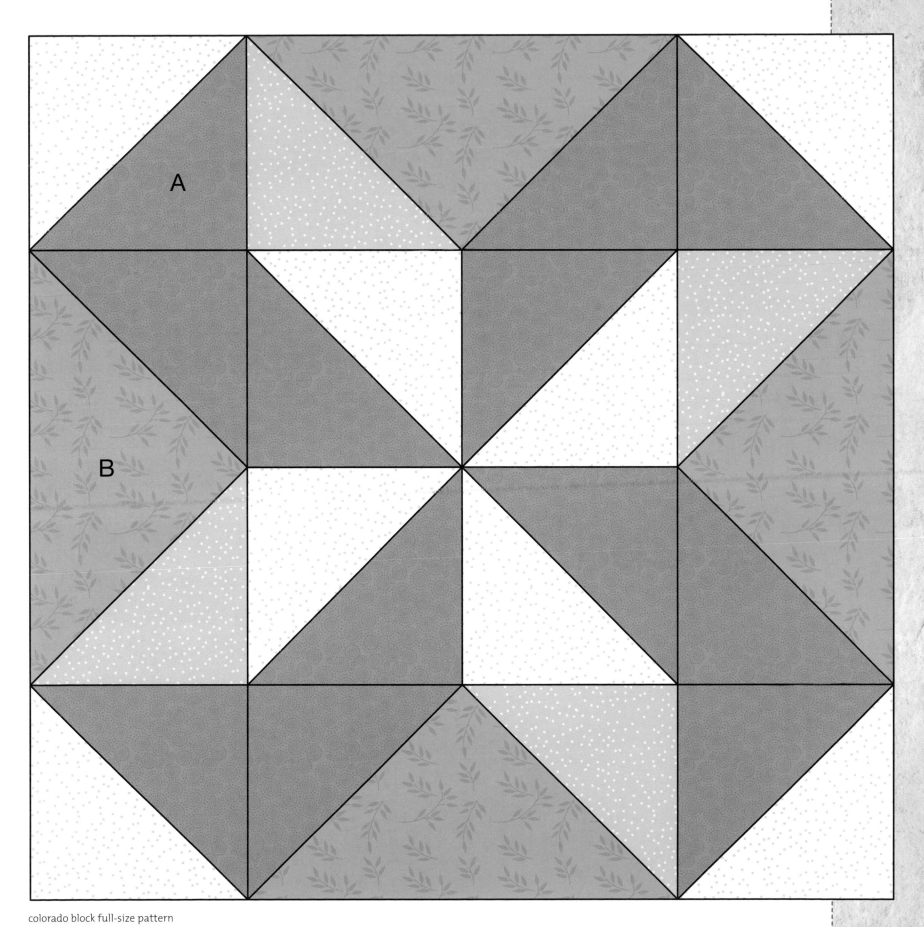

colorado block full-size pattern

four-square

Women came together from all over the state of Minnesota to quilt this traditional pattern for Quilt Pink Day. To see the entire quilt, turn to page 195.

Submitted by Minnesota Quilters Inc.
Minneapolis, Minnesota

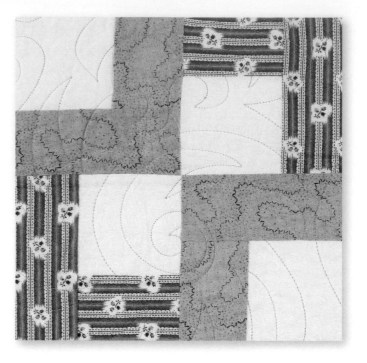

assemble the block

1 Make ABC unit (4 times).
2 Sew units together, rotating each unit.

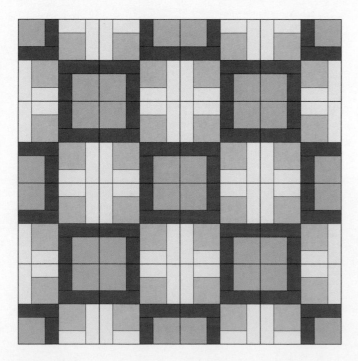

try this

Create a geometric effect by changing color and placement of the blocks.

look again

Sewing the blocks together in rows makes the squares seemingly less organized.

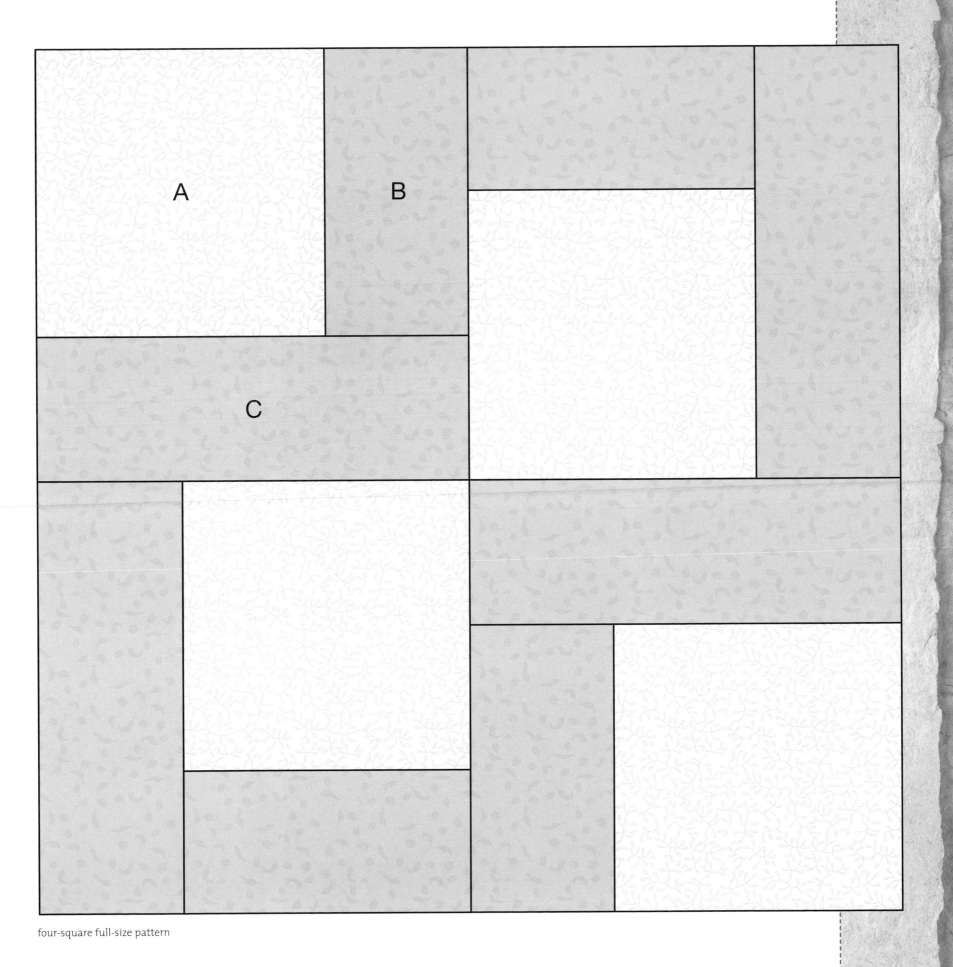

four-square full-size pattern

moo-desto pink cow

Cathie Hoover of Modesto, California, designed this whimsical Moo-desto Pink Cow pattern. Customers at the R Lily Stem Quilts donated $5.00 to the Susan G. Komen for the Cure to receive the pattern. More than $700 was raised and a folk art style quilt was created. To see the entire quilt, turn to page 195.

Submitted by R Lily Stem Quilts
Modesto, California

assemble the block

NOTE: *To order the pattern and instructions in the size shown on the quilt, page 195, visit www.cathiehooverstudios.com.*

1 Make G1G2G3G4G5 unit.

2 Make F1F2F3F4F5 unit.

3 Make B1B2B3B4B5B6B7B8B9 unit.

4 Make C1C2 unit.

5 Make D1D2D3D4D5 unit.

6 Sew G unit to F unit.

7 Sew H to GF unit.

8 Sew C to B unit.

9 Sew D to CB unit.

10 Sew E to DCB unit.

11 Appliqué cow square to background A.

12 Sew ribbon beads and embellishments.

try this

Angle the pieced cow block in different directions for a playful effect.

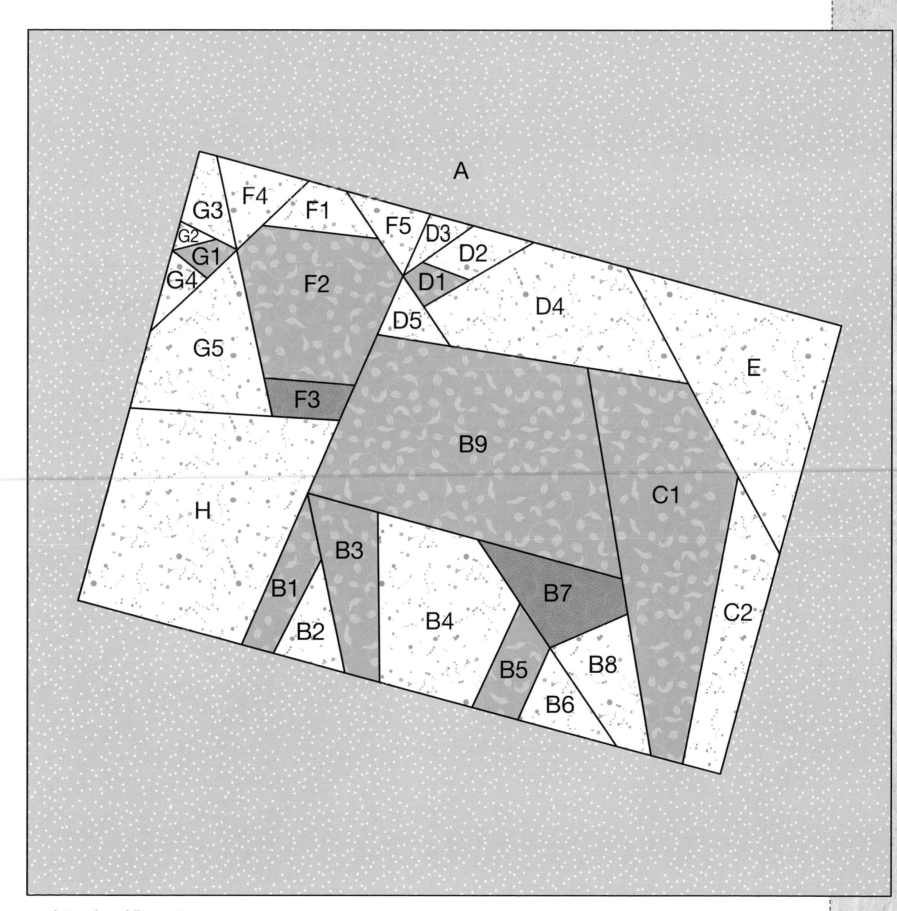

moo-desto pink cow full-size pattern

pinwheel star

The women in this guild chose an all-time favorite block to make their quilt for the cause. To see the entire quilt, turn to page 194.

Submitted by Quilters Unlimited Guild
Mt. Vernon Chapter, Alexandria, Virginia

assemble the block

1 Sew medium B to dark B (4 times) for center.
2 Sew light B to dark B (4 times).
3 Make AABBA unit for Row 1.
4 Make BBBBBBA unit for Row 2.
5 Make ABBBBBB unit for Row 3.
6 Make ABBAA unit for Row 4.
7 Sew rows together.

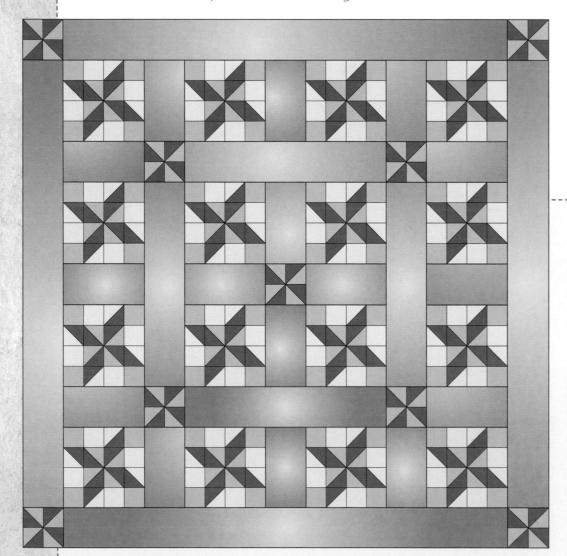

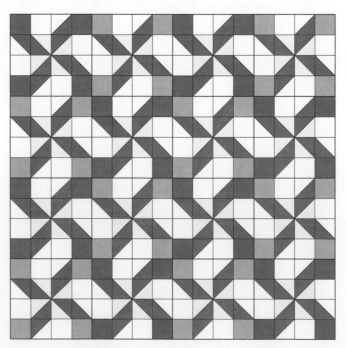

try this

Add pinwheel blocks as sashing and corner squares to create the star blocks.

look again

Sewing the blocks together side by side and changing the color placement makes the design seem to move.

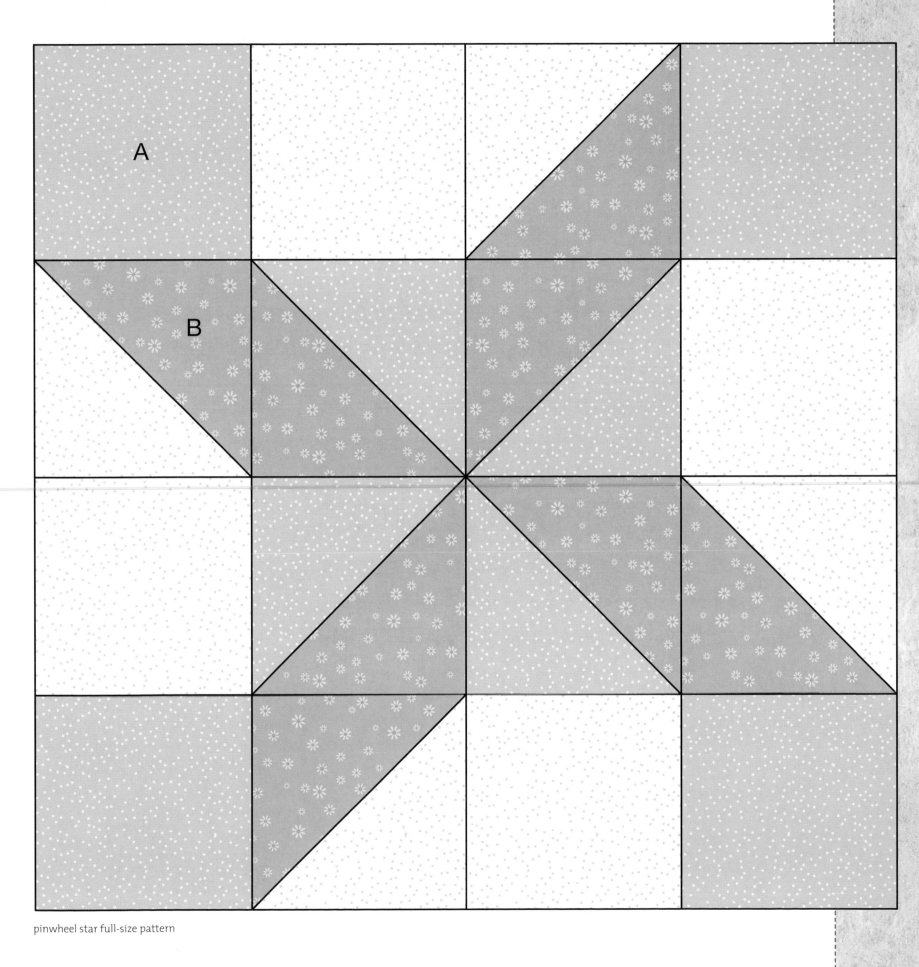

pinwheel star full-size pattern

circle star

This Circle Star block is one of the traditional patterns used in the stunning sampler quilt submitted by Country Quiltworks. To see the entire quilt, turn to page 195.

Submitted by Country Quiltworks
Montgomeryville, Pennsylvania

assemble the block

1 Make CBDCr (4 times).

2 Make ACBDCrA (2 times) to make Rows 1 and 3.

3 Sew E to F (4 times) to make center unit.

4 Sew CBDCr to opposite sides of center unit for Row 2.

5 Sew rows together.

try this

Use two colors and elements from the block for the sashing for a coordinated effect.

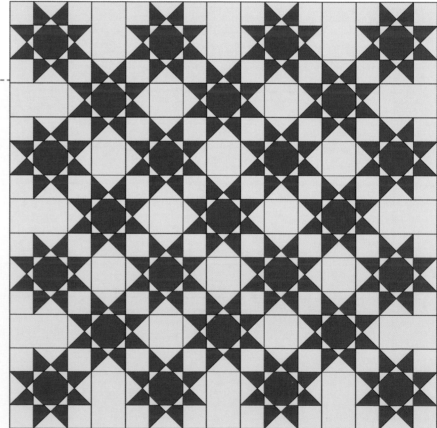

look again

Create a graphic effect by using the side units of the block between the full blocks.

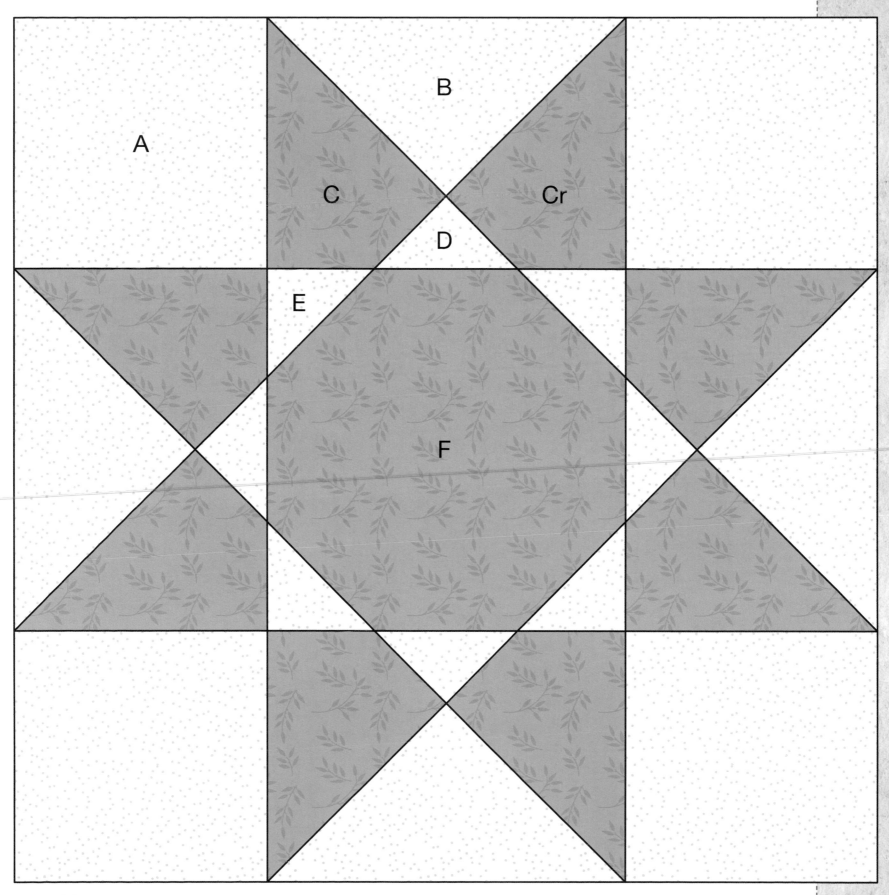

circle star full-size pattern

heart and hand

Patti Kaplan designed this block using her own hand and a simple heart pattern. She says, "It takes both our hearts and our hands to create blocks for the cause." To see the entire quilt, turn to page 196.

Submitted by Calico, Canvas & Colors
Racine, Wisconsin

assemble the block

1 Appliqué hand and heart shapes to background fabric A.

try this

Arrange other heart and flower blocks to create a playful look. Shown here with the Heart and Hand block are the Heart Petals block, page 180, and the Four Hearts block, page 168.

A

heart and hand full-size pattern

crowned cross

The women from Calico Hutch gathered together to make quilts for charity using a favorite block—Crowned Cross. They designed quilts in various colorways, one in retro pink and blue for Quilt Pink. To see the entire quilt, turn to page 196.

Submitted by Calico Hutch
Hayward, Minnesota

assemble the block

1 Make BBC unit (8 times).
2 Sew BBC units to opposite edges of D (4 times).
3 Sew A to opposite sides of BBCDBBC (2 times) to make top and bottom rows.
4 Sew CCCE (4 times).
5 Sew CCCE units together to make center.
6 Sew BBCDBBC units to sides of center.
7 Sew rows together.

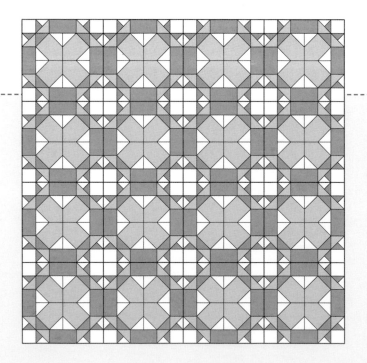

try this

This traditional block can be placed in so many ways with interesting results every time. By simply arranging the blocks side by side, the rectangles on each side form squares that connect the design.

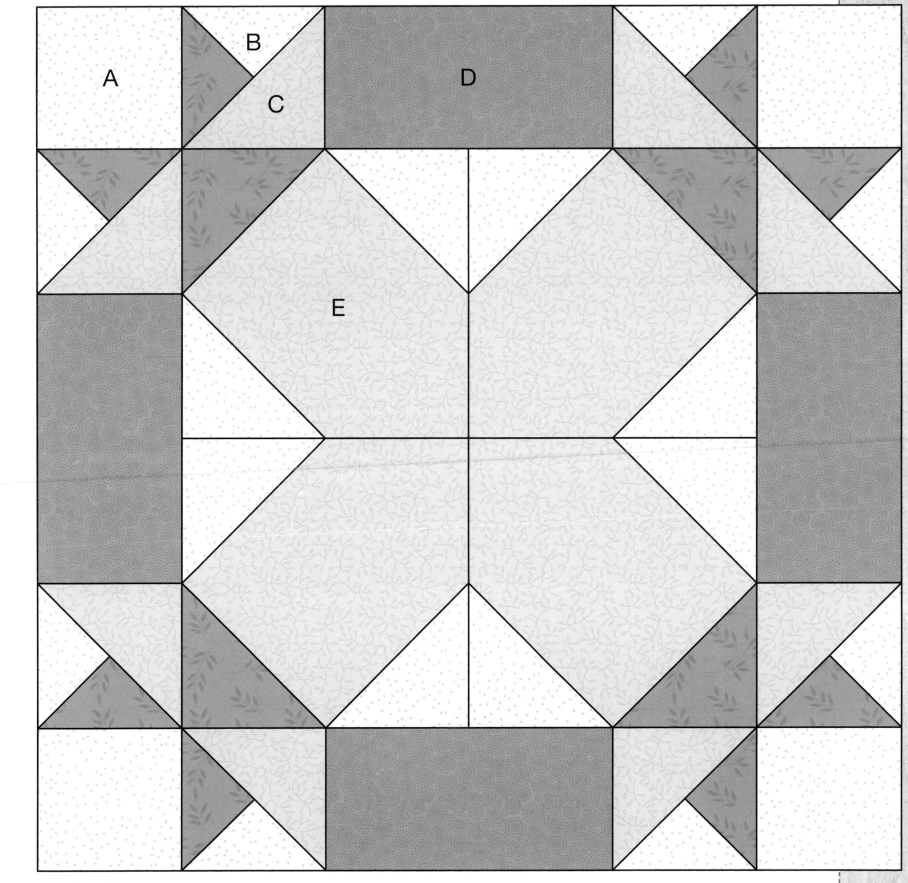

crowned cross full-size pattern

heart quartet

This appliqué heart block is from a sampler quilt from the "Little Old Ladies" of Mt. Vernon. To see the entire quilt, turn to page 194.

Submitted by Quilters Unlimited Guild
Mt. Vernon Chapter, Alexandria, Virginia

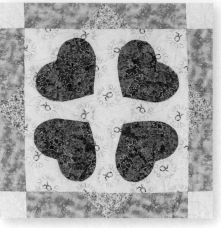

assemble the block

1 Make BCBr unit (4 times).

2 Sew A to opposite ends of BCBr (2 times).

3 Appliqué hearts to D.

4 Sew BCBr units to sides.

5 Sew ABCBrA units to remaining sides.

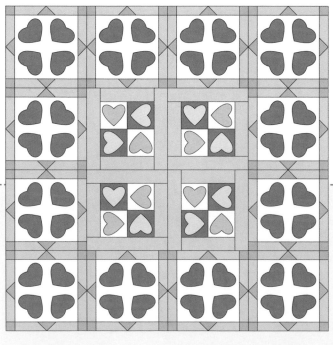

try this

Make a heart-theme quilt using different heart blocks pieced together. Shown here is the Heart Quartet encircling Four Hearts shown on page 168.

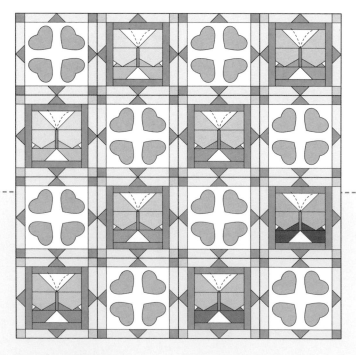

look again

The Pieced Butterfly, page 94, combines with Heart Quartet for a sweet and playful look.

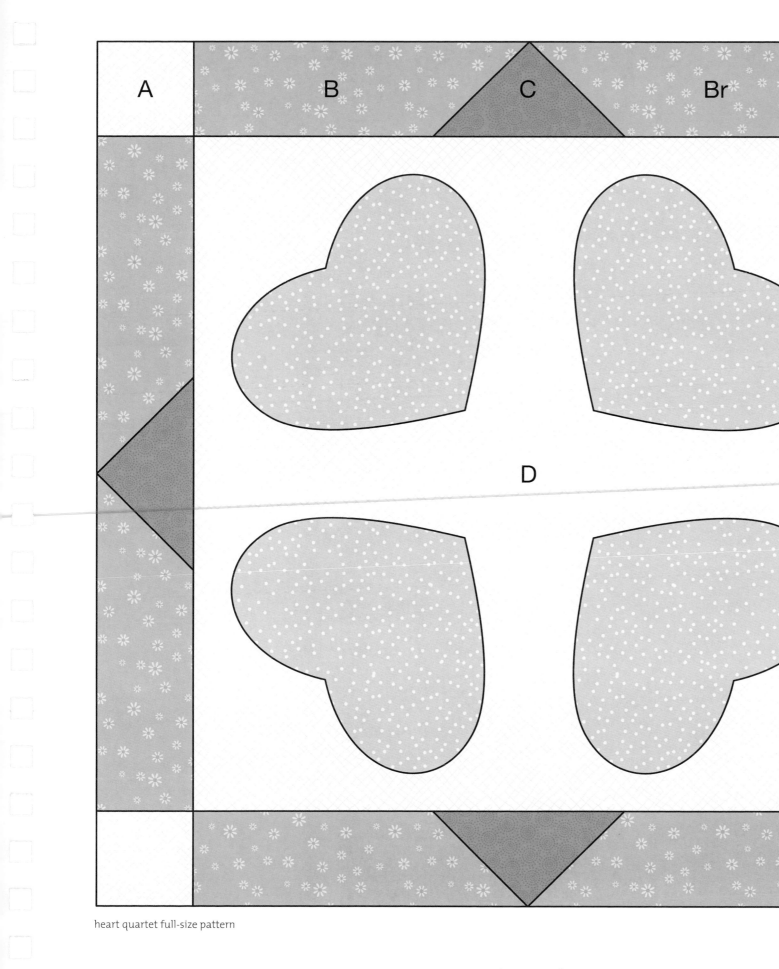

heart quartet full-size pattern

turnabout variation

Jody Carlile, the organizer for Quilt Pink at Debbie's Quilt Shop, created this quilt using a favorite pattern. She made the quilt with her cousin and sister-in-law in mind—both having been diagnosed with breast cancer. To see the entire quilt, turn to page 196.

Submitted by Debbie's Quilt Shop
Paradise, California

assemble the block

1 Make ABB unit (4 times).
2 Sew C unit to ABB unit (4 times).
3 Sew four units together.

try this
Sashing, with squares of the fabric used in the blocks, gives a swirling design to this quilt top.

look again
Place the blocks side by side using a colorful palette for a burst of energy.

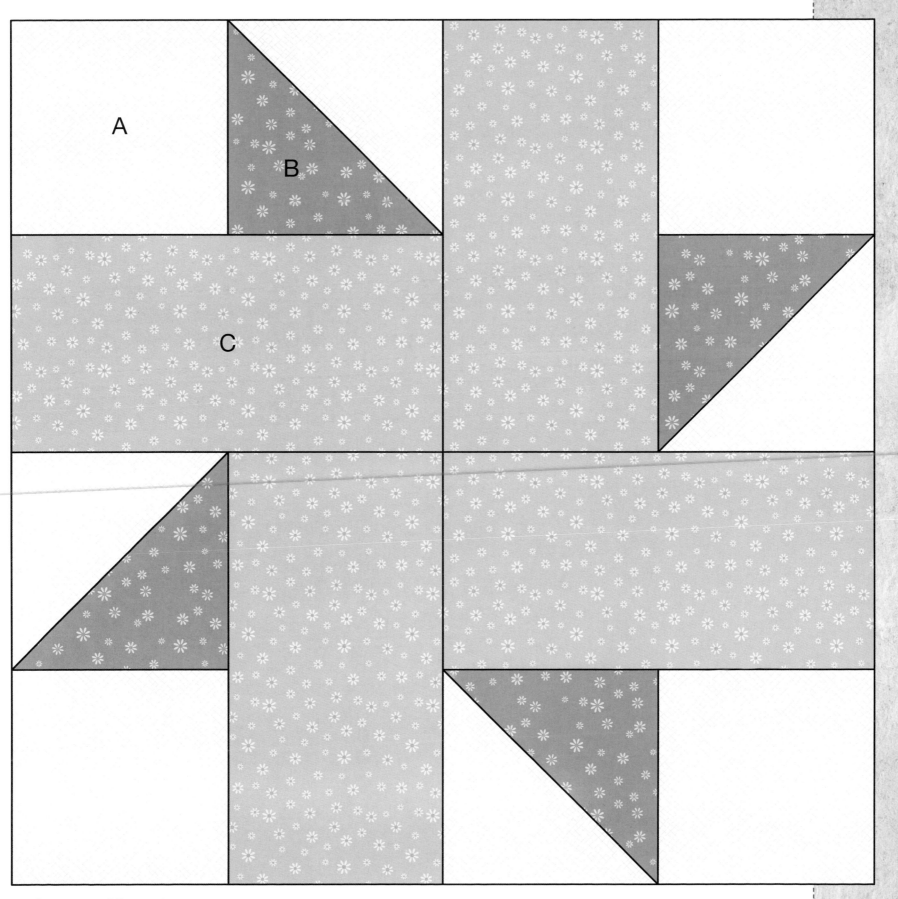

turnabout variation full-size pattern

king's crown

Debra Staley, owner of Quilters Workshop and her friend Sandi are both great NASCAR fans. They shared this interest as they worked on a quilt together during Sandi's treatment. To see the entire quilt, turn to page 195.

Submitted by Quilters Workshop
Oak Harbor, Washington

assemble the block

1 Make BAB unit (4 times).
2 Sew units to sides of C.

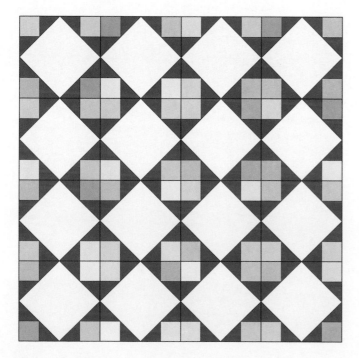

try this
Use a light-color fabric for the center diamond and then make it a signature quilt.

look again
Combine two different blocks for striking results. Shown here with Kings' Crown is the Colorado Block, page 98.

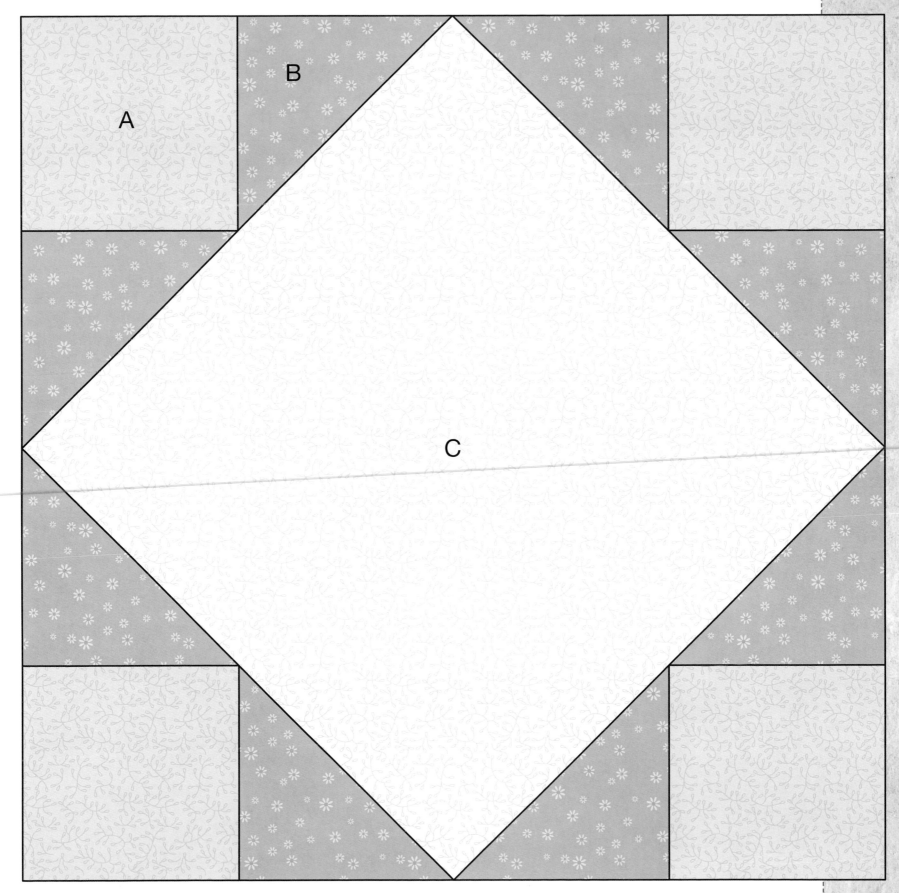

king's crown full-size pattern

t-block variation

Quilted by Teddy Wuertz of Dayton, Minnesota, the Stripy T quilt was completed for Quilt Pink and proudly hung with many other beautiful quilts in the atrium at the Mall of America. Then it was donated to raise money for fighting breast cancer. To see the entire quilt, turn to page 196.

Submitted by Quilted Treasures
Rogers, Minnesota

assemble the block

1 Make BCB unit (4 times).

2 Sew D to BCB unit (4 times)

3 Make AA unit (4 times).

4 Sew an AA unit to opposite sides of BCBD unit (2 times), to make Rows 1 and 3.

5 Sew BCBD units to opposite sides of E square.

6 Sew rows together, reversing last row.

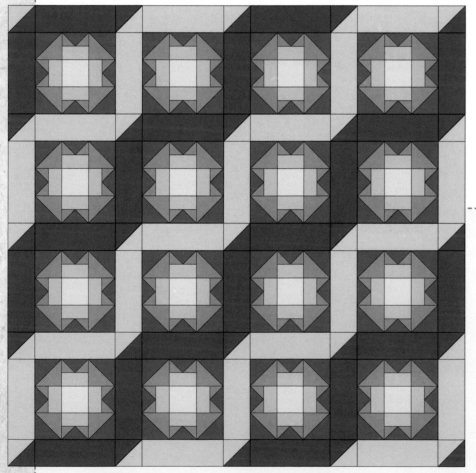

try this

Laying out the blocks with two-color pieced sashing suggest a running ribbon frame for the blocks.

look again

Turning the blocks on point and abutting them forms new square-in-a-square blocks.

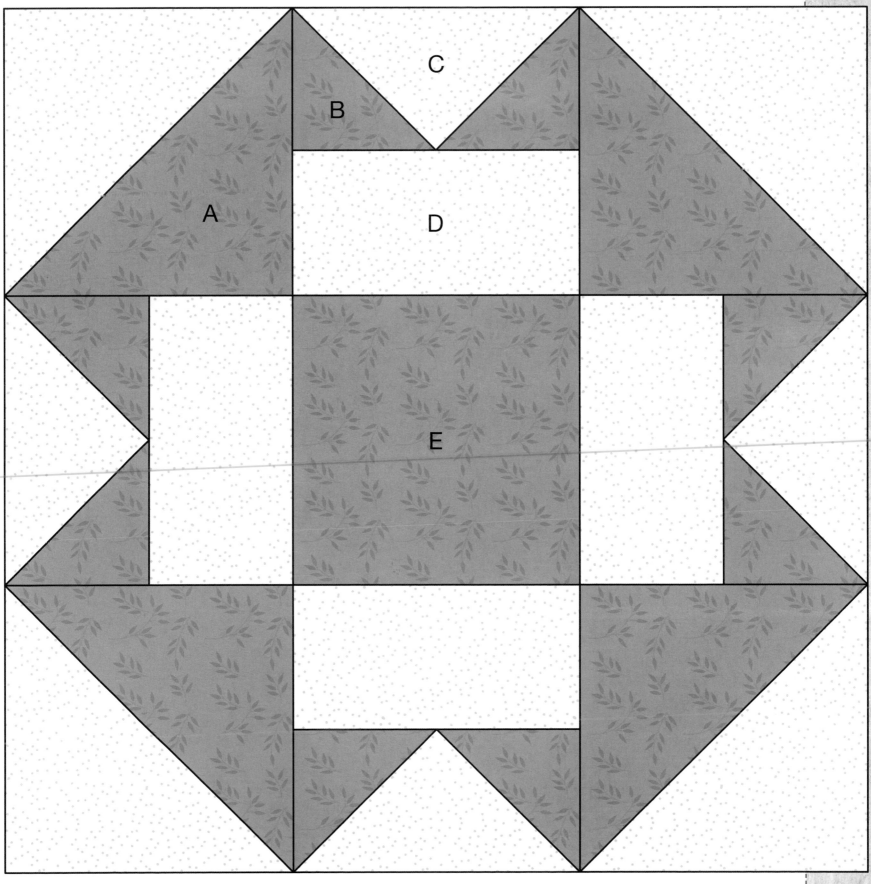

t-block variation full-size pattern

rose of sharon nine-patch

This traditional Rose of Sharon block was made by Kate Gollsneider in honor of her mother, Sharyn, a breast cancer survivor. To see the entire quilt, turn to page 197.

Submitted by And Sew It Goes
Savage, Maryland

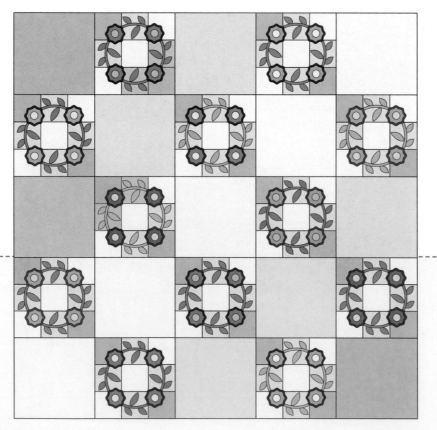

assemble the block

1 Make a Nine-Patch using the A squares.
2 Appliqué leaves and stems first.
3 Appliqué flowers next.
4 Appliqué flower centers last.

try this

This elegant block stands alone, especially when it has the added interest of the Nine-Patch. Choose subtle, light-color setting squares between the blocks to set off the beauty of the appliqué.

A

rose of sharon nine-patch full-size pattern

geometric bows

This quilt made by Carol Majerus was dedicated to two members of the staff at Eagle Creek Quilt Shop, Jane Ward and Becky Kelso. Both women are breast cancer survivors. To see the entire quilt, turn to page 197.

Submitted by Eagle Creek Quilt Shop
Shakopee, Minnesota

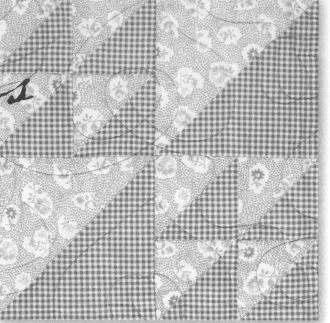

assemble the block

1 Make AA (8 times).
2 Make AAAAAAAA unit (2 times).
3 Make BB unit (2 times).
4 Sew units together.

try this

Rotate the block to form a group of four blocks. Continue until desired size of quilt is achieved.

look again

With the blocks joined side by side, the lights and darks create the popular sunlight and shadows effect.

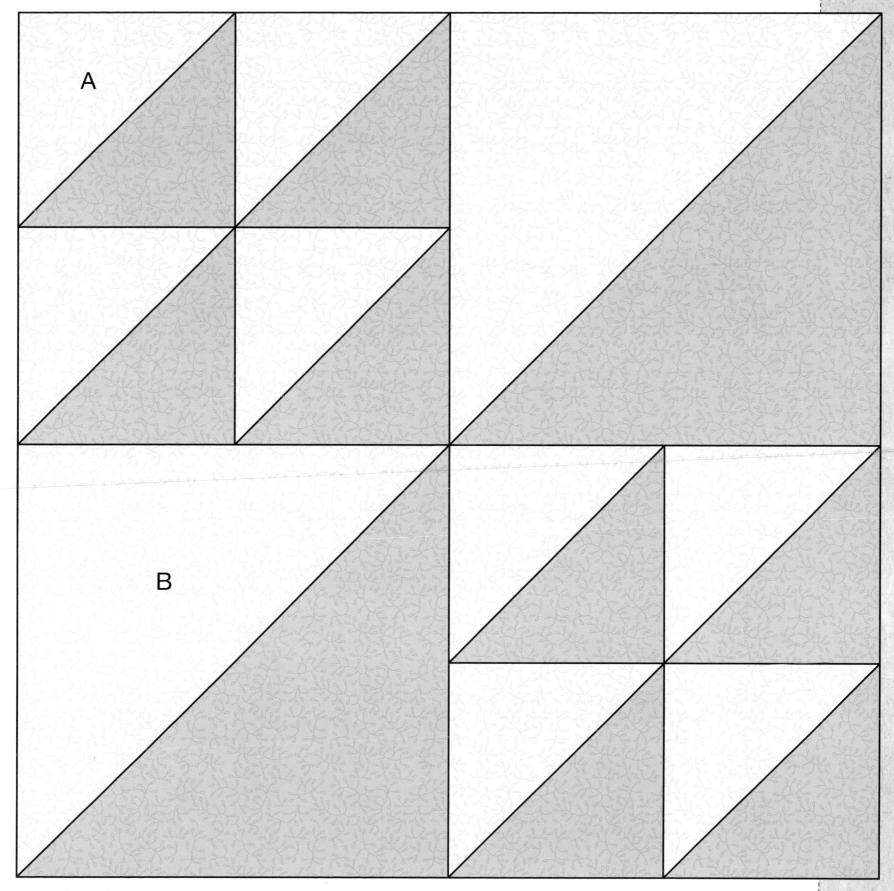

geometric bows full-size pattern

windmill

Long Island Quilters Society is a non-for-profit organization dedicated to furthering interest in quilting. Long Island, New York, has been identified as an area with a very high incidence of breast cancer, and these women were proud to be a part of Quilt Pink. To see the entire quilt, turn to page 197.

Submitted by Long Island Quilters Society
Mineola, New York

assemble the block

1 Make ABC unit (4 times).
2 Make CD unit (4 times).
3 Join ABC unit and CD unit to form a square (4 times).
4 Join squares to make a Four-Patch.

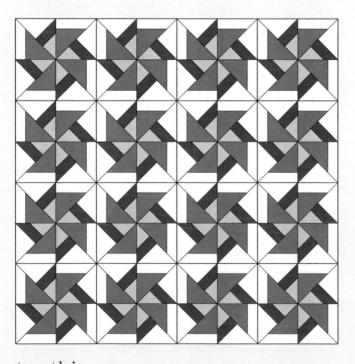

try this

Laying out the blocks side by side without sashing emphasized a feeling of movement or windmills turning.

look again

Rotating the position of the quarters suggests thin-bladed pinwheels separated by diamonds.

windmill full-size pattern

delectable mountain variation

This traditional block design with its many pieces offers opportunity to use a variety of pink fabrics. It was submitted by Quilters Unlimited from Alexandria, Virginia. To see the entire quilt, turn to page 194.

Submitted by Quilters Unlimited Guild
Mt. Vernon Chapter, Alexandria, Virginia

assemble the block

1 Make BB unit (16 times).
2 Make ABBBBBBBBBA unit (2 times).
3 Sew D to sides of E (4 times).
4 Sew C to DED unit (4 times) to create center unit.
5 Sew BBBBBBBB units to opposite sides of center unit.
6 Sew ABBBBBBBBBA units to top and bottom of center unit.

try this

Combine a variety of patchwork designs in all shades of pink. The blocks used here with Delectable Mountain Variation are Prairie Queen, page 188; T-Block Variation, page 118; and Mosaic, page 156.

look again

Simply placing the blocks side by side creates patterns that form faux sashing.

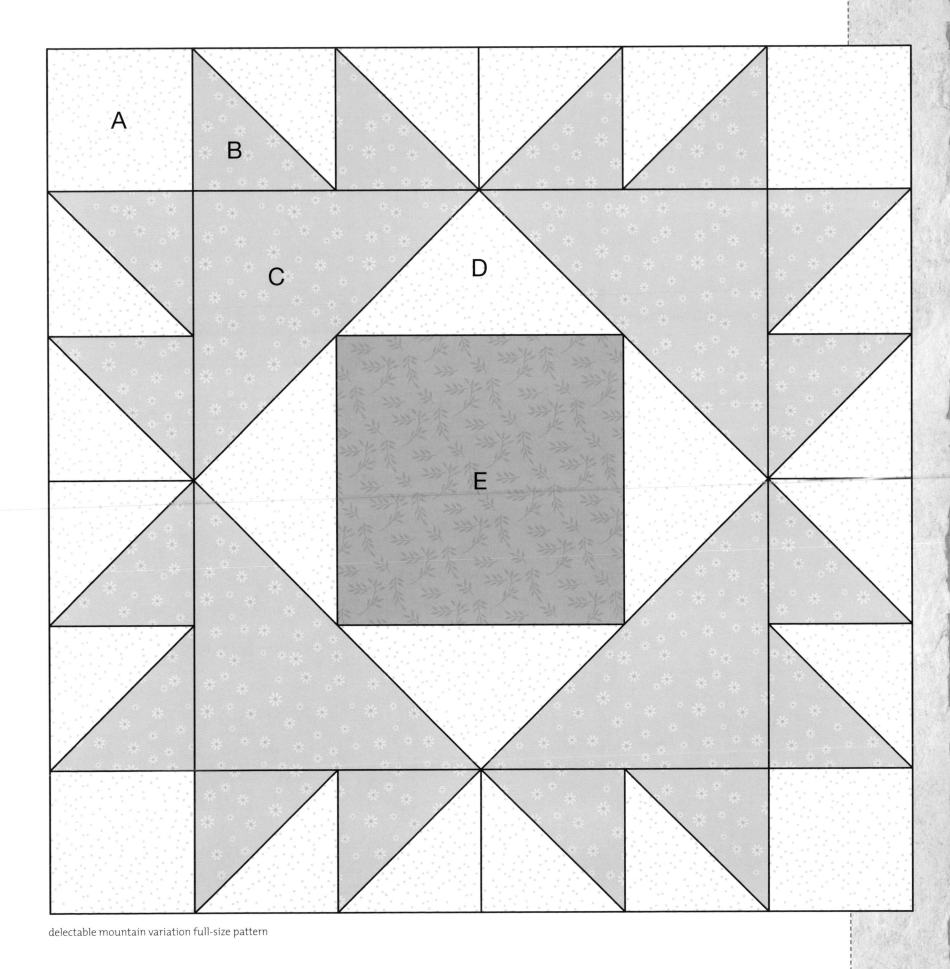

delectable mountain variation full-size pattern

center cross

A Canadian quilt group made a sampler quilt for the cause. This block is one of those in the finished quilt. To see the entire quilt, turn to page 197.

Submitted by A Quilter's Heart
Grimsby, Ontario, Canada

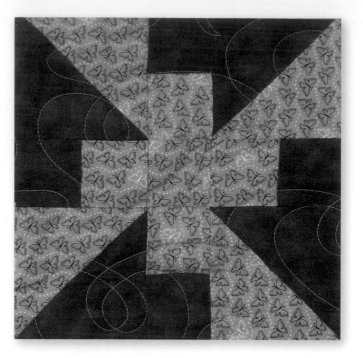

assemble the block

1 Make AA unit (4 times).
2 Make AABCAA unit (2 times) for Rows 1 and 3.
3 Make BCCCB for center row.
4 Sew rows together.

try this
Sashing, using same size pieces as the center row, looks like lattice strips.

look again
The triangles appear as pinwheels when the blocks are placed side by side.

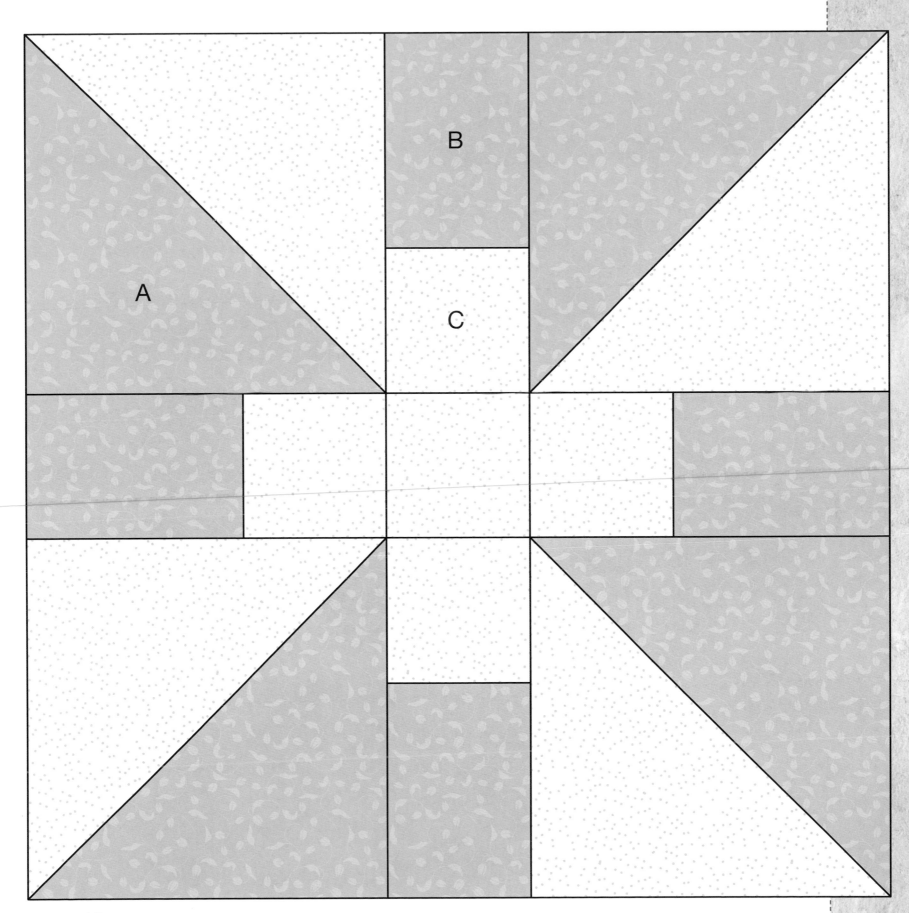

center cross full-size pattern

friendship star

Friendship is a strong theme in guild meetings at the Just Friends Guild in Colo, Iowa. Announcements about marriages, divorces, and health crises are the norm. The Friendship Star block seemed appropriate for this close-knit group of quilters. To see the entire quilt, turn to page 198.

Submitted by Just Friends Quilt Guild
Colo, Iowa

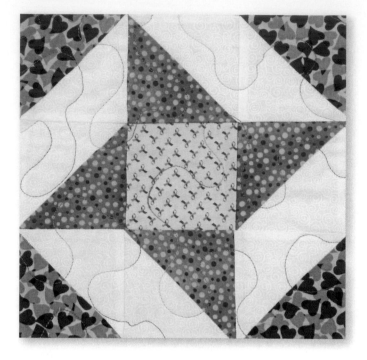

assemble the block

1 Make AA (light, dark) unit (8 times).
2 Sew AAAAAA (2 times) for Rows 1 and 3.
3 Sew AABAA for Row 2.
4 Sew rows together.

try this
Combine this block with the Card Tricks block, page 132. Make the Card Tricks block in a one-color variation.

look again
When pieced side by side, the block creates its own grid of diagonal shapes.

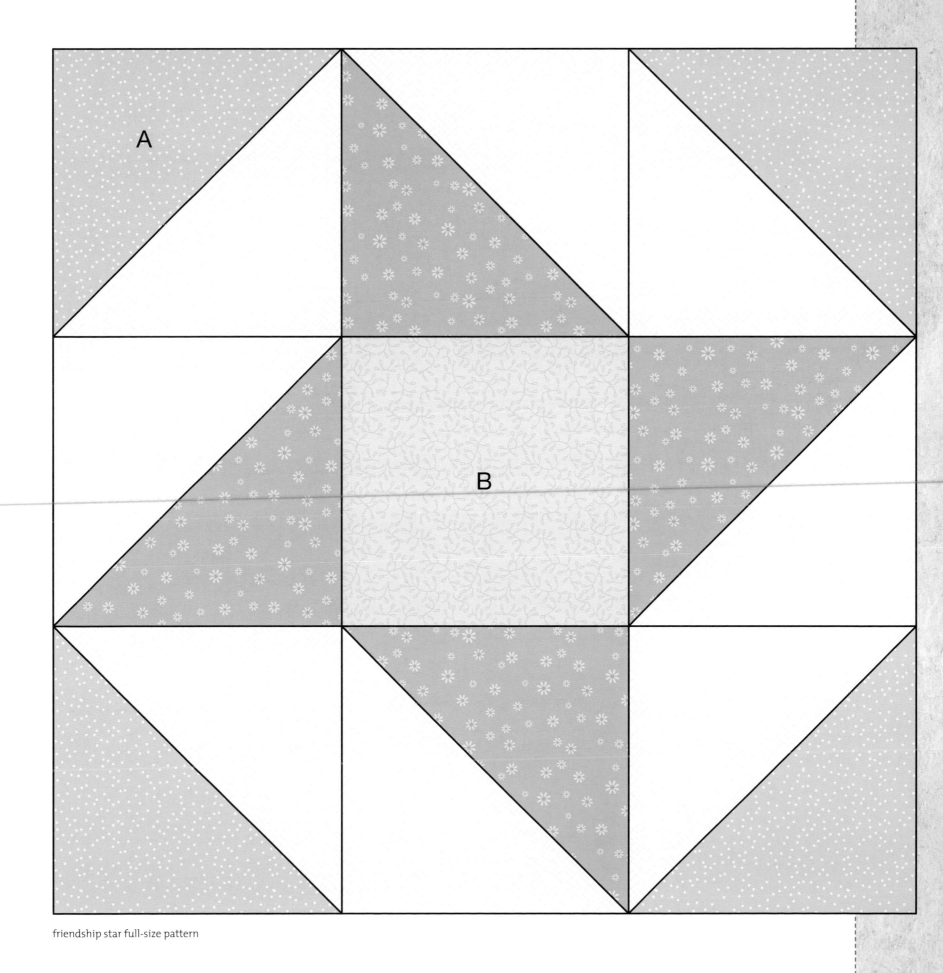

friendship star full-size pattern

card tricks

The members of a quilt shop in Las Vegas thought it would be fun to make a pink quilt using the favorite Card Tricks block. To see the entire quilt, turn to page 198.

Submitted by Fabric Boutique Quilt Shop, Las Vegas, Nevada

assemble the block

1 Make AA unit (4 times).
2 Make ABB unit (4 times).
3 Make BBBB for center unit.
4 Sew AAABBAA (2 times) for Rows 1 and 3.
5 Sew ABBBBBBABB for Row 2.
6 Sew rows together.

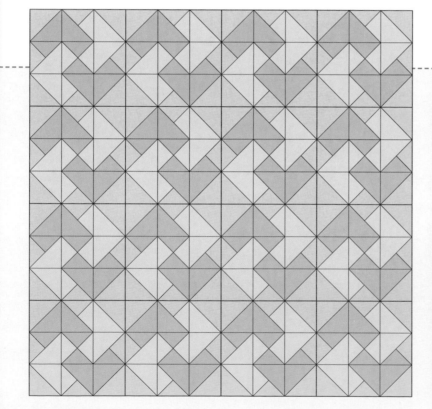

try this
Assembling the blocks side by side with no sashing creates a diamond in the center of every group of four.

look again
Laying the blocks on point creates a visual twist.

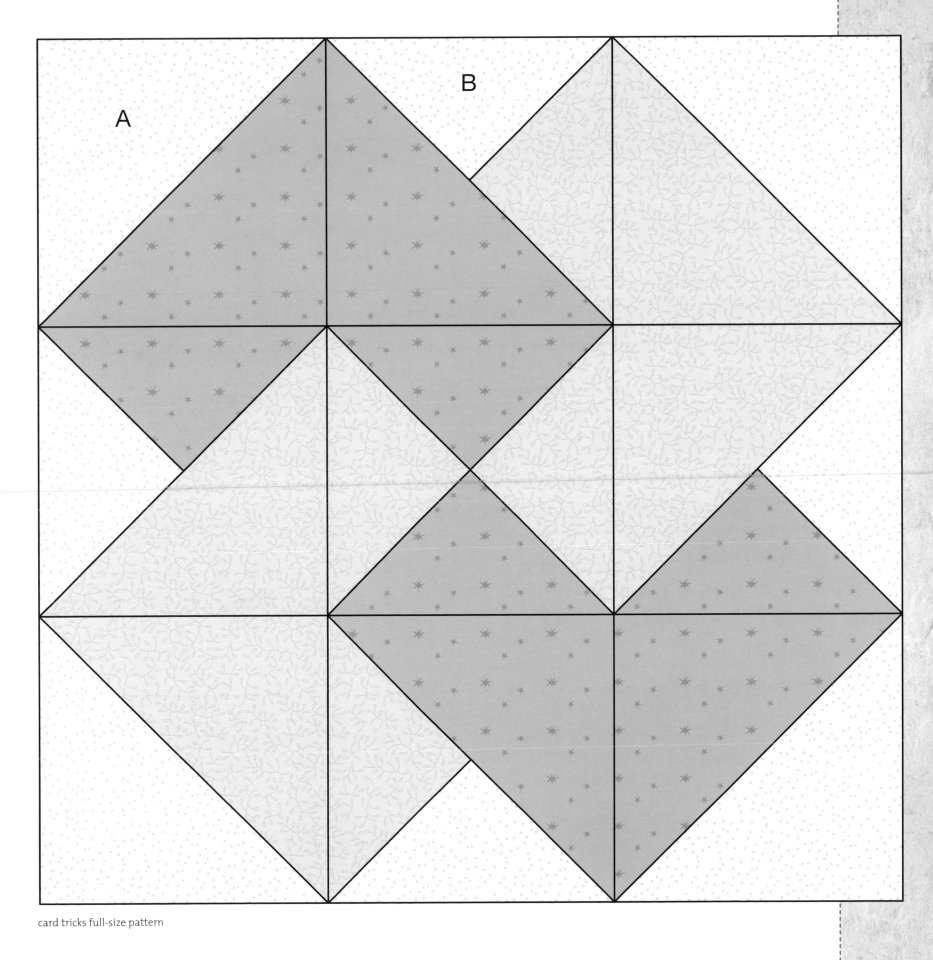

card tricks full-size pattern

royal star

High-contrast fabric makes this star sparkle. It stands out on the sampler quilt made by the dedicated quilters from Beaumont, California. To see the entire quilt, turn to page 198.

Submitted by Georgia's Quilting Obsession
Beaumont, California

assemble the block

1 Make AB unit (4 times).
2 Make DE unit (4 times).
3 Sew C to DE unit (4 times).
4 Sew F to CDE unit (4 times).
5 Sew CDEF to AB unit (4 times).
6 Sew four units together.

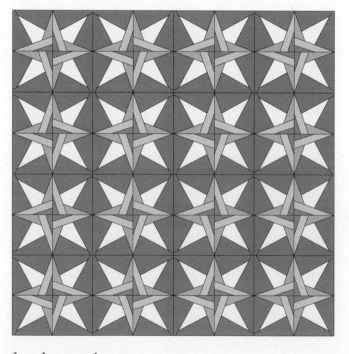

look again

Placing the blocks side by side makes each block pop and appear three-dimensional.

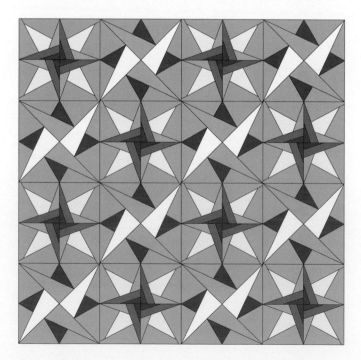

try this

The quilt idea shown here combines two star blocks, Royal Star and Dimensional Star, page 170.

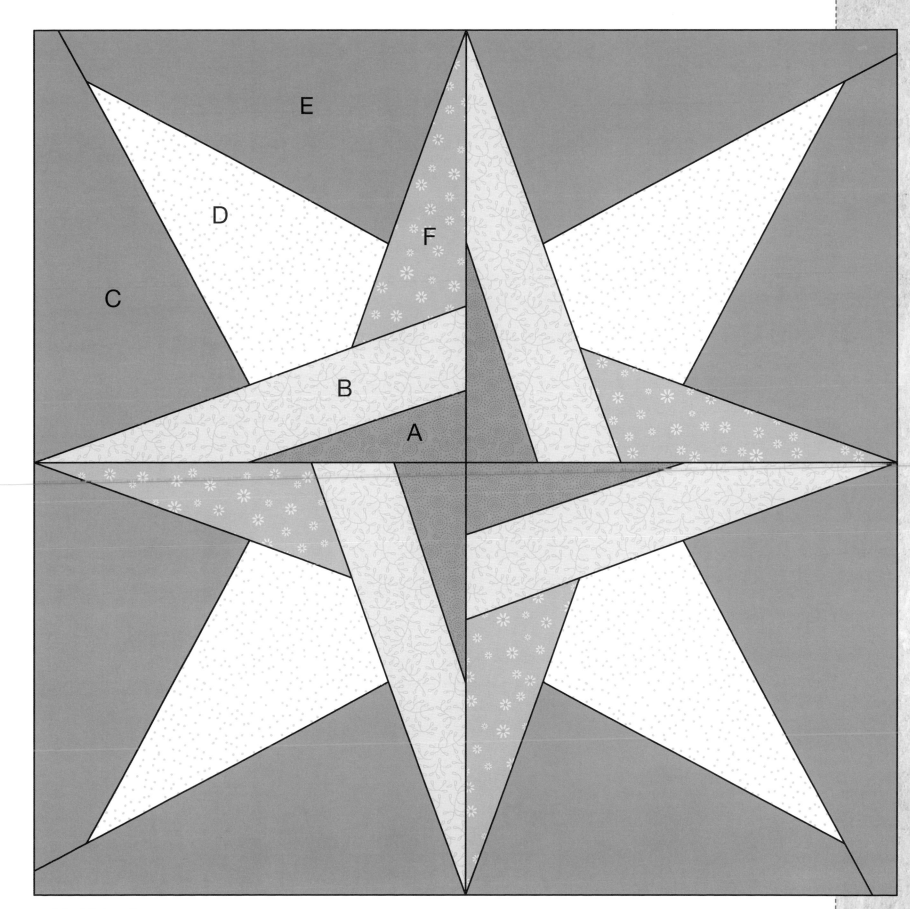

royal star full-size pattern

love umbrella

Ciré Gray designed this umbrella block to convey that rain creates a shower of love falling over the umbrella. The mother-of-pearl button on the handle represents her mother, who passed away from cancer years ago. To see the entire quilt, turn to page 198.

Submitted by Quilt Lounge and Knittery
Deer Park, Washington

assemble the block

1 Appliqué handle in place to background fabric A.
2 Appliqué umbrella pieces.
3 Appliqué raindrops.
4 Sew on bow and button if desired.

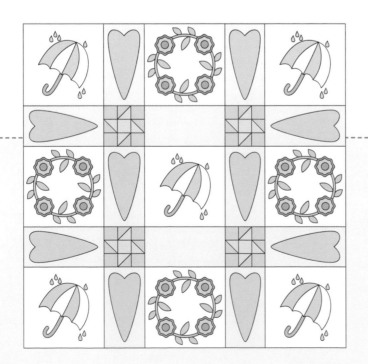

try this

Combine whole and half blocks for a clever and playful effect. The blocks shown here with Love Umbrella are Rose of Sharon Nine Patch, page 120, and Heart and Star, page 154.

A

love umbrella full-size pattern

log cabin square

Linda Green, owner of Calico Canvas & Colors, says, "Breast cancer touches all women, which is why I believe our customers donated so many blocks. It has been a wonderful experience for us as shop owners." To see the entire quilt, turn to page 196.

Submitted by Calico, Canvas & Colors
Racine, Wisconsin

assemble the block

1 Sew pieces together beginning with AA and building to D (4 times).
2 Sew 4 units together.

look again

Log Cabin blocks form many wonderful and beautiful designs depending on the lights and darks of the fabrics and where they are placed.

try this

The Log Cabin squares become the border when the middle of the quilt is a different block. The center block shown is Triangle Block, page 176.

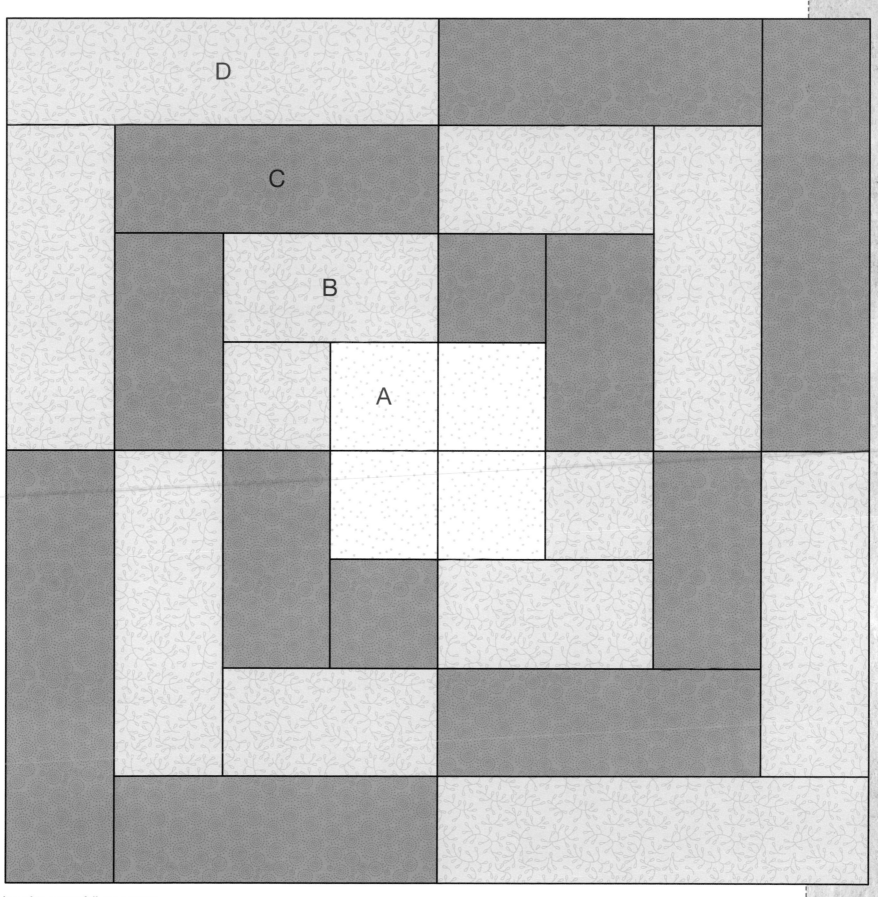

log cabin square full-size pattern

bear's paw

The women in this group of quilters from Ontario, Canada, chose the Bear's Paw quilt block pattern as one of many in their sampler quilt. To see the entire quilt, turn to page 197.

Submitted by A Quilter's Heart
Grimsby, Ontario, Canada

assemble the block

1 Make AA unit (16 times).
2 Sew AAAA unit to B (4 times).
3 Make AAAAC unit (4 times).
4 Sew BAAAAunit to AAAAC unit (4 times).
5 Sew units together.

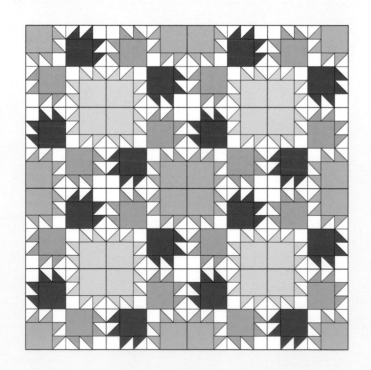

try this

Plan color placement so when the blocks are rotated a larger shape repeats across the finished piece.

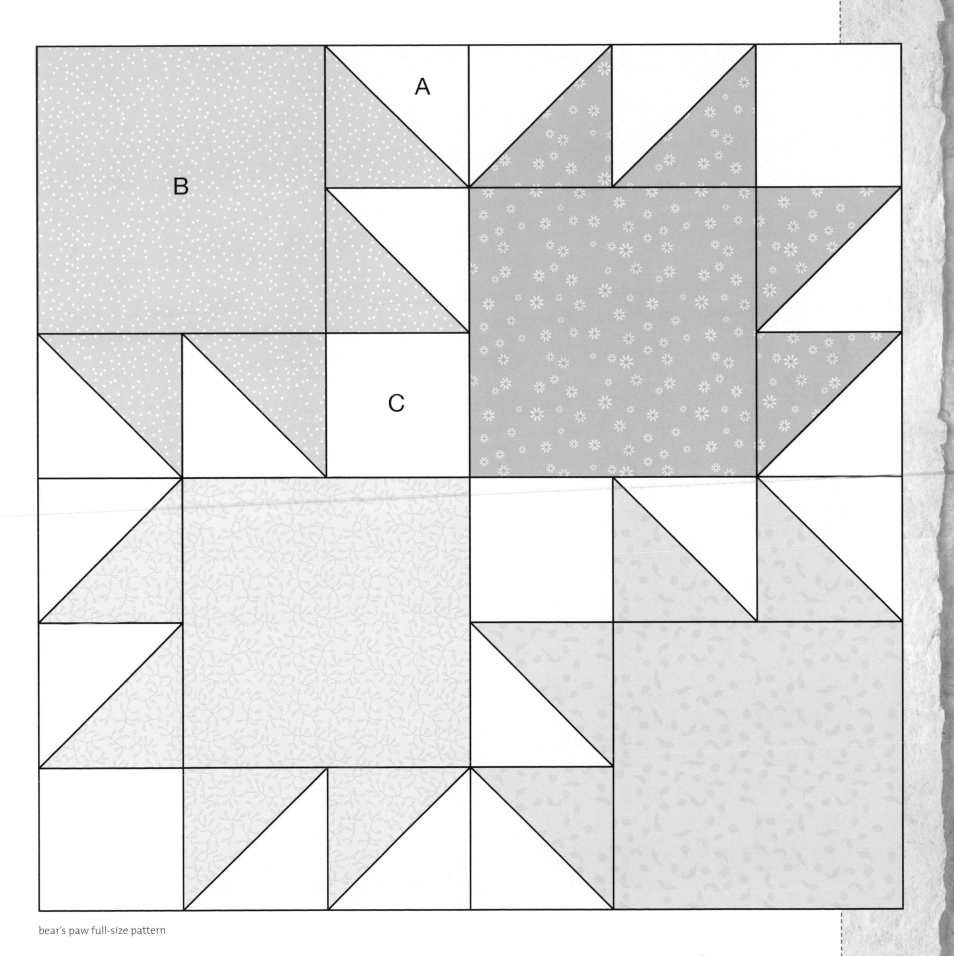

bear's paw full-size pattern

indiana rose

The Indiana Rose is a beautiful classic block. It was chosen for the sampler quilt sent in by the women at In Stitches located in Rushville, Indiana. To see the entire quilt, turn to page 199.

Submitted by In Stitches Quilt Shop
Rushville, Indiana

assemble the block

1 Appliqué to background fabric A.
2 Appliqué flowers first, then leaves.
3 Appliqué center flower and center last.

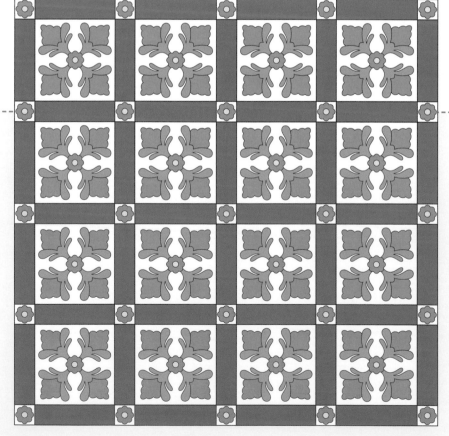

try this

Use the center of the rose pattern to embellish the corner blocks that link the sashing strips. The sashing strips are the same value as the block colors but are a different color, making the block stand out as a framed piece.

A

indiana rose full-size pattern

whirling pink

This Whirling Pink block was created by the Jackson Hole Quilt Guild. The quilting on the finished piece is done with machine-quilted petals over the pieced block. To see the entire quilt, turn to page 199.

Submitted by Stitch 'N Time
Jackson, Wyoming

assemble the block

1 Make ABAr (4 times).
2 Make ABArCABAr(2 times) for Rows 1 and 3.
3 Make CDC for Row 2.
4 Sew rows together.

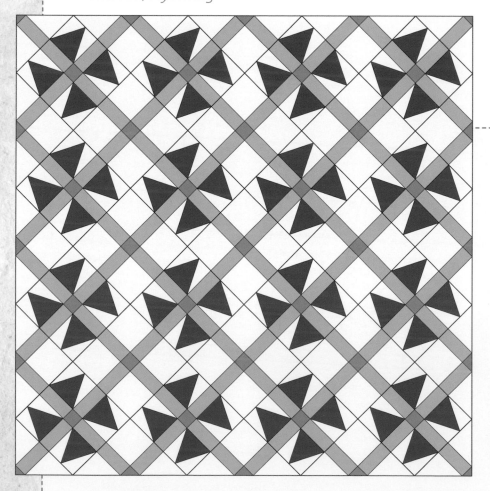

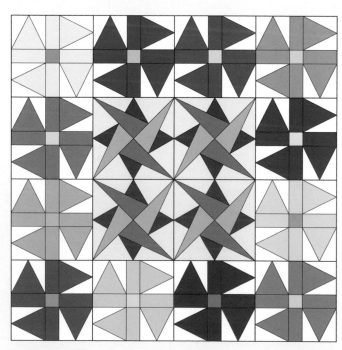

try this
Set on point with alternating squares, the blocks gain prominence.

look again
Combining Whirling Pink with Dimensional Star, page 170, produces a lively swirl of color and shape.

whirling pink full-size pattern

ohio star variation

Evelyn Larrison designed and incorporated two traditional blocks, the Four-Patch Chain and the Ohio Star, to make this block for Quilt Pink. To see the entire quilt, turn to page 199.

Submitted by Walcott Sewing & Vacuum Madison, Wisconsin

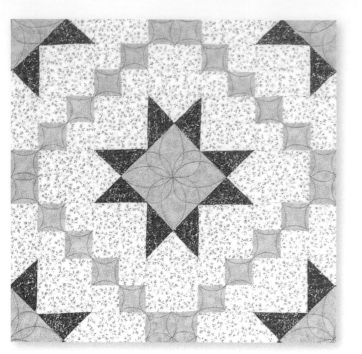

assemble the block

1 Make ABCBCD (4 times).
2 Make FFFF (8 times).
3 Sew E to FFFF (8 times).
4 Sew EFFFF to D (4 times).
5 Sew ABCBCDEFFFF to EFFFFD (4 times).
6 Sew B1B1B1B1 (4 times).
7 Sew E1D1B1B1B1B1 (4 times).
8 Sew E1D1B1B1B1B1 to each side of center D1.
9 Sew units together.

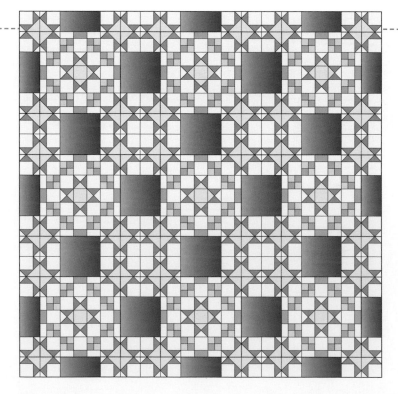

try this

Piecing Ohio Star Variation block corners with large solid squares creates a secondary, interwoven block.

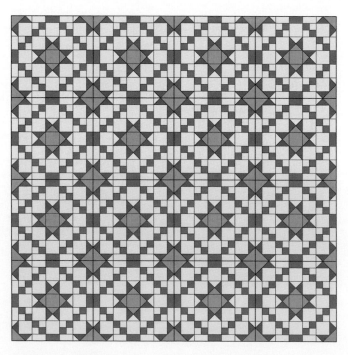

look again

Straight-set blocks form connecting stairsteps.

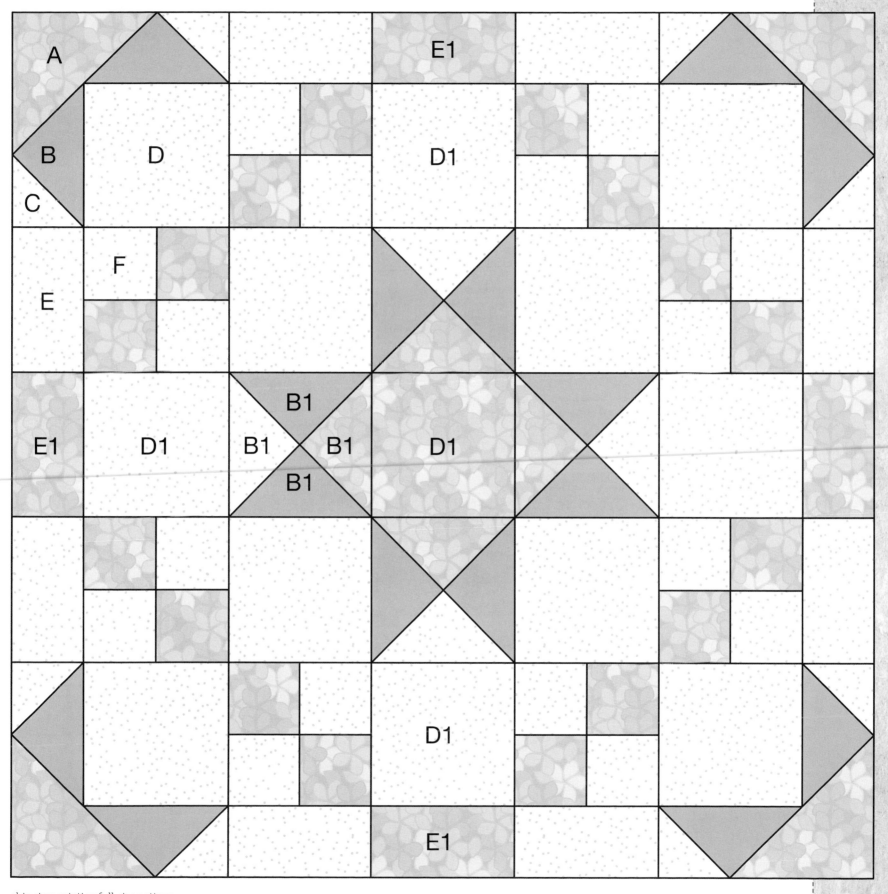

ohio star variation full-size pattern

friendship star variation

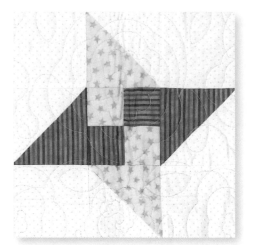

The quilters from Country Quiltworks used the Friendship Star Variation as one of the blocks in their sampler quilt. To see the entire quilt, turn to page 195.

Submitted by Country Quiltworks
Montgomeryville, Pennsylvania

assemble the block

1 Make AAAA center unit.
2 Make BB unit (4 times).
3 Sew CBBC unit (2 times) for Rows 1 and 3.
4 Sew BBAAAABB to make Row 2.
5 Sew rows together.

try this

Combine similar blocks to create a pleasing effect. The quilt design shown here uses the Friendship Star Variation block and the Friendship Star, page 130.

look again

Placing the blocks side by side and changing colors gives a sense of structure and order to the quilt.

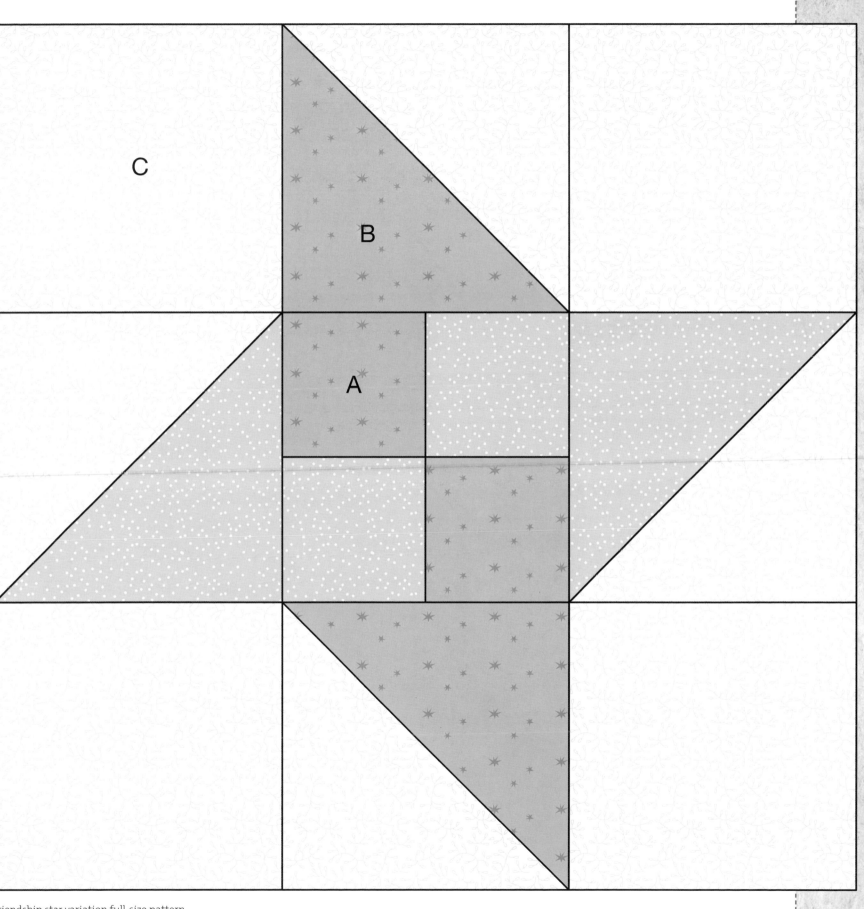

friendship star variation full-size pattern

pink basket

Susan Cooper of the Quilt Lounge says, "My shop was only five months old when I sent out the word about Quilt Pink. We received more than 80 blocks. We just played with the blocks until the quilt took shape." To see the entire quilt, turn to page 198.

Submitted by Quilt Lounge and Knittery
Deer Park, Washington

assemble the block

1 Make BB unit (3 times).
2 Join in vertical rows adding single B piece to bottom of each row.
3 Join rows, adding a B piece to complete the section.
4 Sew to A.
5 Make DB unit (2 times). Sew to adjacent sides of A.
6 Sew C to make corner.

try this
Set four Pink Basket blocks together to form a graphic pattern in the center.

look again
Combine Pink Basket with Four-Square, page 100, for a stunning geometric diagonal look.

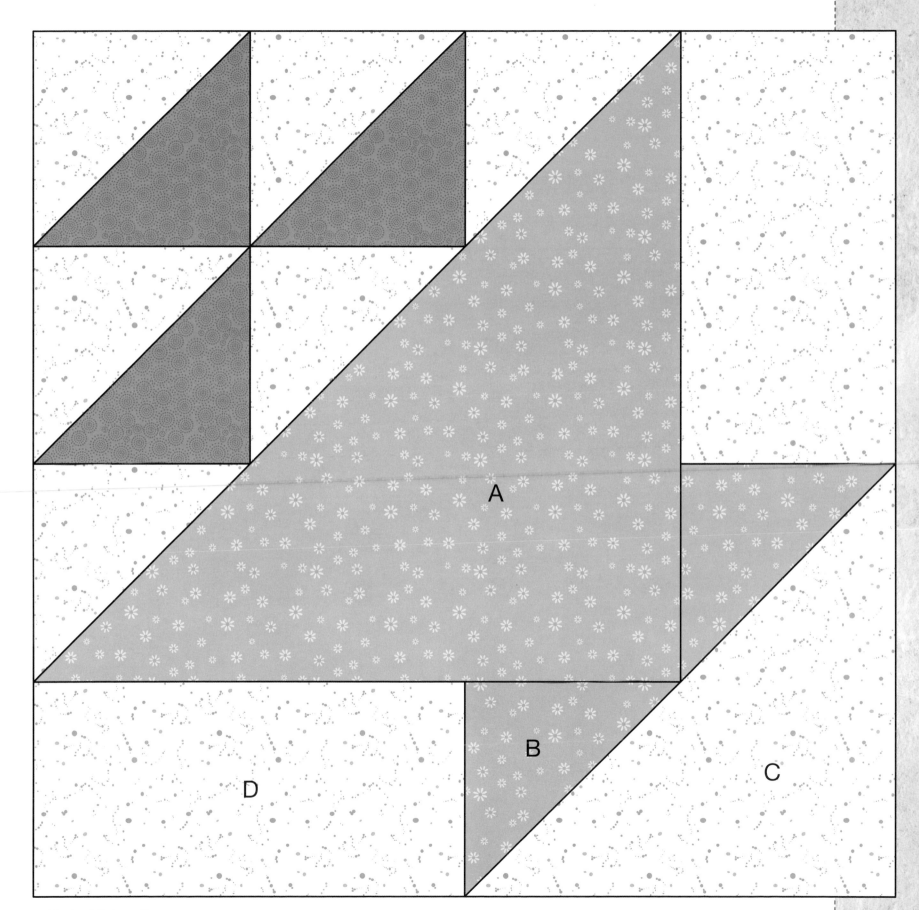

pink basket full-size pattern

geometric heart

Timeless Treasures of McGregor, Minnesota, used a simple shape to represent their love. To see the entire quilt, turn to page 199.

Submitted by Timeless Treasures
McGregor, Minnesota

assemble the block

1 Make ABA unit (2 times)
2 Make CC unit (2 times)
3 Sew ABA units together. Sew CC units together.
4 Sew sections together.

look again
With the hearts connected in a row and then inverted, diamonds form along the horizontal seams.

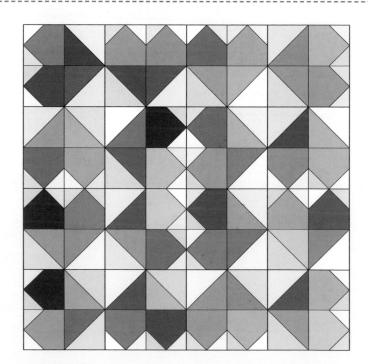

try this
Turning some of the hearts sideways and upside down results in a variety of backround shapes.

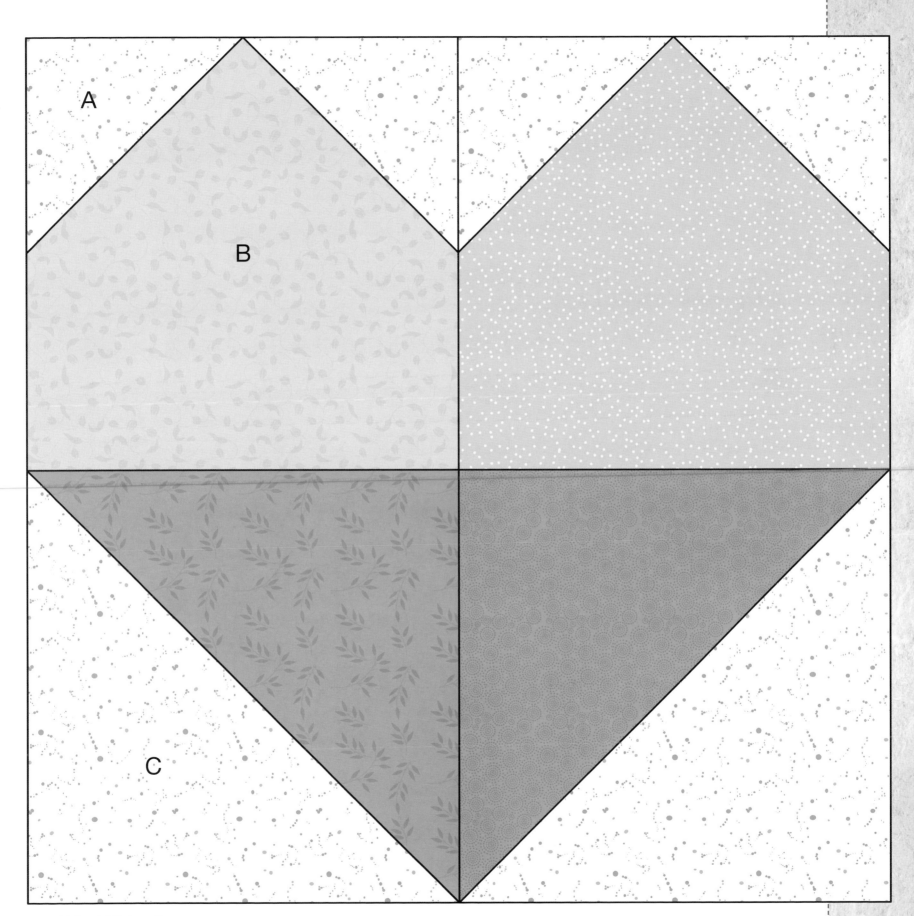

geometric heart full-size pattern

heart and star

The women at Fabric Corner wanted to make a quilt that people of every level of quilting expertise could participate in. Collen Janssen of Fabric Corner says, "It is amazing how efforts that involve women tend to bring so many people together for such a worthy cause, and far exceeds the original expected outcome." To see the entire quilt, turn to page 200.

Submitted by Fabric Corner
Topeka, Kansas

assemble the block

1 Appliqué heart to background fabric A for Unit 1.
2 Make BBBB Four-Patch for Unit 2.
3 For Unit 3: Make DD (4 times).
4 Make CDDC (2 times) for Rows 1 and 3.
5 Make DDCDD for Row 2.
6 Sew rows together. Sew units together.

try this

Alternate the star unit with the Four-Patch unit for a fun alternative that gives movement to the stars.

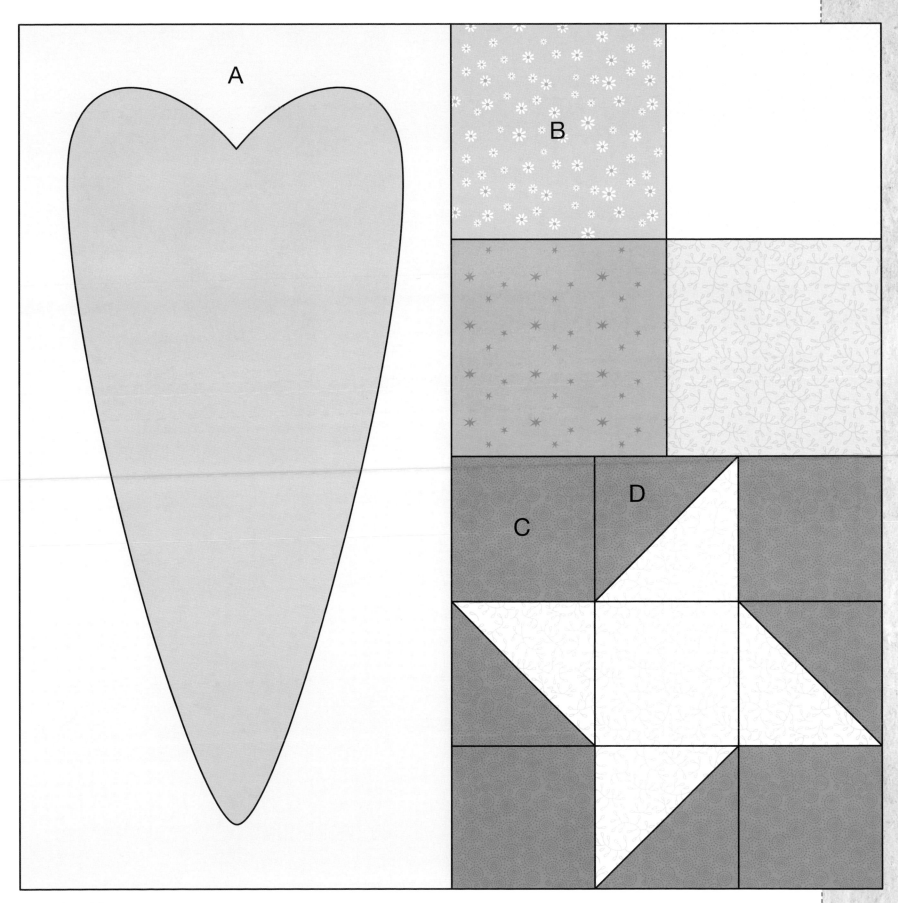

heart and star full-size pattern

mosaic

Judy McIlvaine of The Quilt Shop writes, "We are a small shop in the White Mountains of New Hampshire. Customers from all over the area donated their time and effort to make the blocks. We received more than 100 blocks in all." To see the entire quilt, turn to page 200.

Submitted by The Quilt Shop & Vac 'n & Sew Conway, New Hampshire

assemble the block

1 Make AA unit (36 times).
2 Sew units together in rows, arranging lights and darks as indicated on pattern.

try this

Blocks made in several shades of the same color palette and set on point have a kaleidoscope effect.

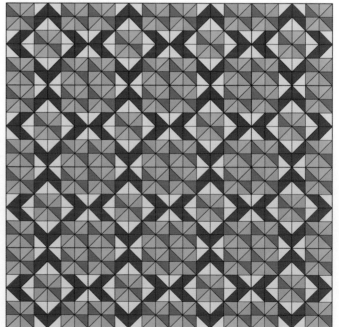

look again

With straight-set blocks in jewel-tone colors, pinwheels come to the foreground while frames recede.

mosaic full-size pattern

appliqué rose

Margaret Mitchell, who began quilting only a few years ago, created this lovely rose block. A retired nurse, Margaret saw many people fight the battle with cancer. To see the entire quilt, turn to page 199.

Submitted by In Stitches Quilt Shop
Rushville, Indiana

assemble the block

1 Begin with the leaves, then layer outer petals and flower center, and finally the petals that appear turned open, appliquéing each piece separately, centered on background fabric A.

2 Embroider the veins in the leaves.

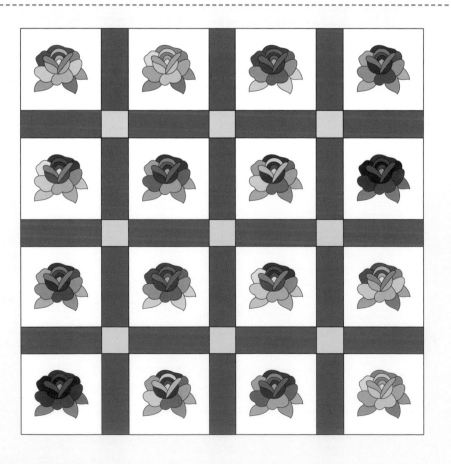

try this

Wide sashing with contrasting sashing squares gives prominence to each appliquéd rose, setting each off as if in a lattice framework.

A

appliqué rose full-size pattern

combination star

This traditional block was one of 30 blocks in a well-coordinated sampler quilt of pink. To see the entire quilt, turn to page 196.

Submitted by Calico, Canvas & Colors
Racine, Wisconsin

assemble the block

1 Make BAB unit (4 times).
2 Make BCB unit (4 times).
3 Sew BAB to BCB unit (4 times).
4 Sew D to opposite sides of BABBCB unit (2 times).
5 Sew B to all sides of E to make center block.
6 Sew BABBCB unit to opposite sides of center unit (2 times).
7 Sew sections together.

try this

Set on point, the star becomes less dominant as it turns on its side and other designs appear.

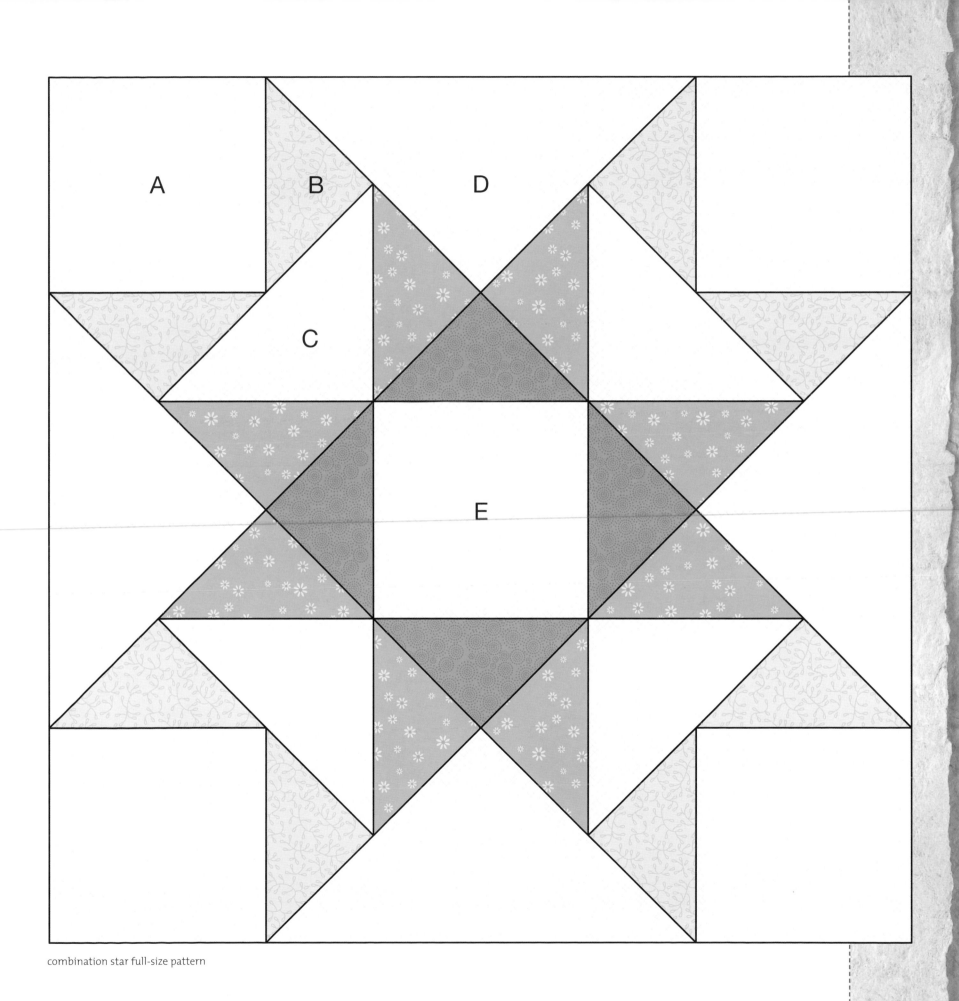

combination star full-size pattern

basket of hearts

Edna DeFord hand-stitched this pretty appliquéd basket of flowers for the friendship sampler by Cotton Fields Quilt & Knit shop. Each staff member made a quilt block to advertise the day and customers came to quilt on Quilt Pink Day, enjoying cookies with pink frosting. To see the entire quilt, turn to page 200.

Submitted by Cotton Fields Quilt & Knit Avondale, Arizona

assemble the block

1 Appliqué the stems first, then the basket to background fabric A.

2 Next appliqué the leaves and flower heart petals.

3 Finally appliqué the center flower buds.

try this

Setting blocks of confetti-style appliquéd hearts made from flower heart petals combine with wide sashing to make a crisp combination.

A

basket of hearts full-size pattern

starflower

Fabric placement makes this Starflower block look like set-in piecing, but it's easy—all squares and half-square triangles. To see the entire quilt, turn to page 200.

Submitted by Stitcher's Crossing
Madison, Wisconsin

assemble the block

1 Make 4 BB units using light and medium, 4 BB units using light and dark, and 4 BB units using medium and dark

2 Make ABBBBA unit for Rows 1 and 4.

3 Make BBBBBBBB (2 times) for Rows 2 and 3.

4 Sew rows together.

try this
When this block is pieced in various colors and blocks are placed side by side, they form a stunning geometric piece.

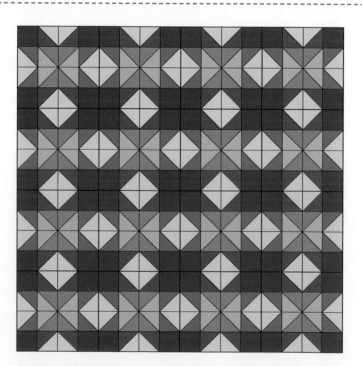

look again
This quilt is pieced exactly the same way. Careful color placement results in an orderly, high-contrast quilt.

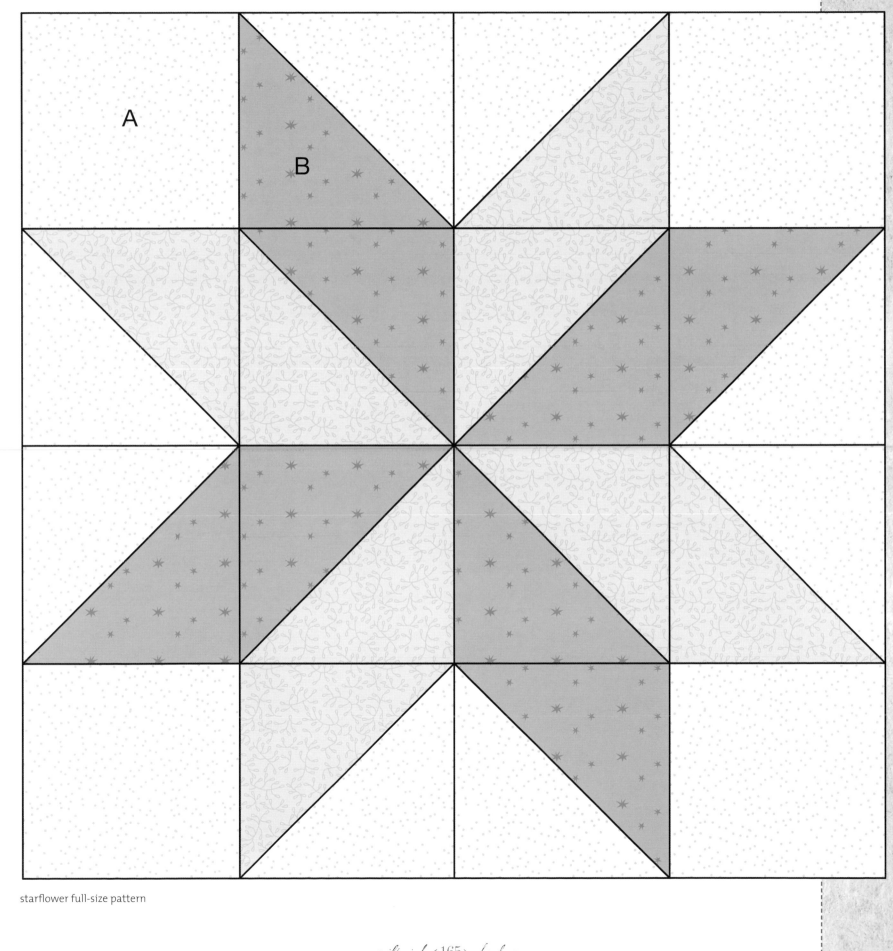

starflower full-size pattern

tree of life

The Tree of Life block seemed appropriate as a block of hope. It was stitched in pink by Margaret Mitchell from Greenfield, Indiana. To see the entire quilt, turn to page 199.

Submitted by In Stitches Quilt Shop
Rushville, Indiana

assemble the block

1 Make BB unit (24 times).
2 Sew F to E and F to Er.
3 Sew FE and FEr to opposite sides of G.
4 Sew D to opposite sides of EFGErF for trunk section.
5 Assemble BB units with A to make top 3 horizontal rows adding single B at end of each row.
6 Join rows to make top section.
7 Sew C to diagonal of top section.
8 Make left section in 3 vertical rows and join the rows sewing single B at bottom of each row.
9 Add C to diagonal of bottom section.
10 Join left section to trunk section.
11 Sew top section to bottom section.

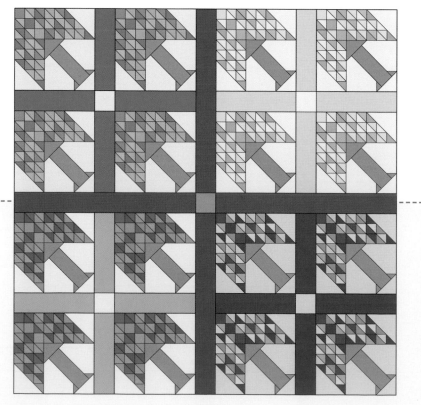

try this

This Tree of Life quilt is designed in quadrants to reflect the four seasons—winter, spring, summer, and fall.

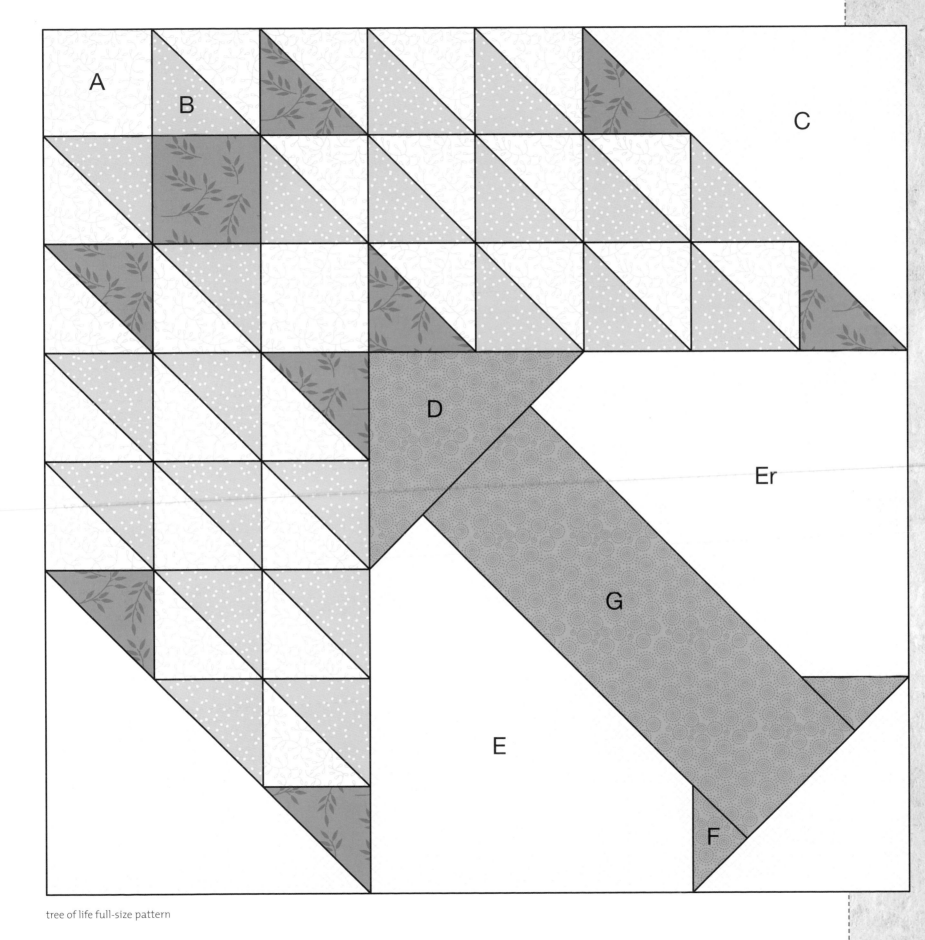

tree of life full-size pattern

four hearts

Pretty in pink, this block is one of 16 in the sashed sampler contributed by staff and customers from The Quilt Shop. To see the entire quilt, turn to page 201.

Submitted by The Quilt Shop & Vac 'n Sew Conway, New Hampshire

assemble the block

1 Appliqué hearts to background fabric C (4 times).

2 Sew together for center unit.

3 Sew B to opposite sides of center unit.

4 Sew A to remaining sides.

try this

Combine flowers and hearts to make a cheerful quilt. The blocks shown here with Four Hearts are Heart Quartet, page 112, Basket of Hearts, page 162, and Three Flowers, page 190.

try this

Appliqué hearts to the sashing squares. Set the heart blocks with solid-colored squares between the Four Hearts blocks.

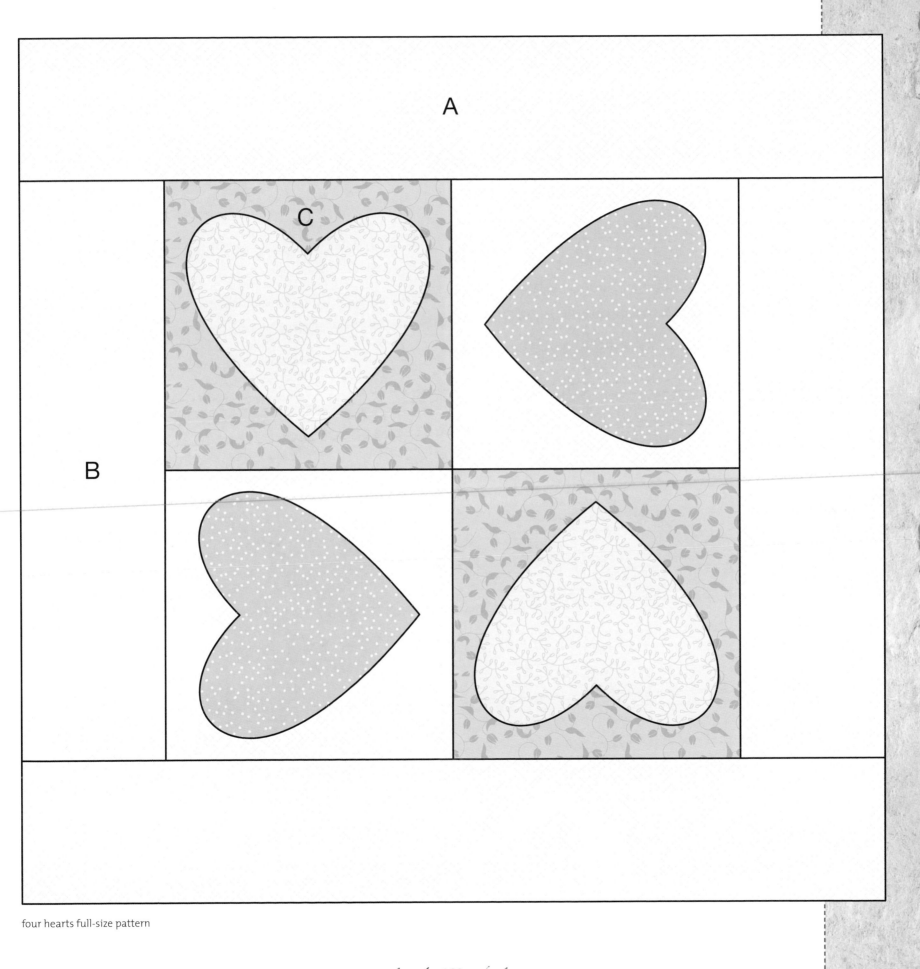

four hearts full-size pattern

dimensional star

This Dimensional Star block is just one of the beautiful blocks in a sampler quilt submitted by A Quilters Heart. To see the entire quilt, turn to page 197.

Submitted by A Quilters Heart
Grimsby, Ontario, Canada

assemble the block

1 Make ABCD unit (4 times).
2 Sew units together.

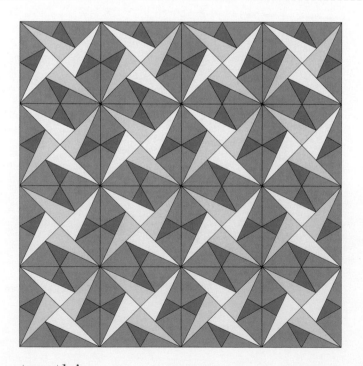

try this

This quilt is full of energy when blocks are set in straight rows.

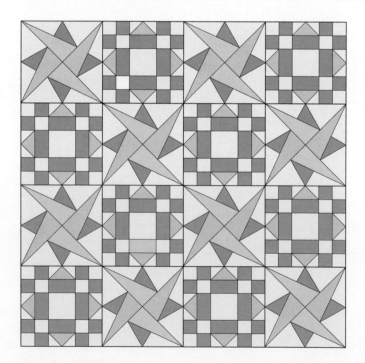

look again

Combining Dimensional Star with Diamond in a Square block, page 178, makes a stunning combination of color and pattern.

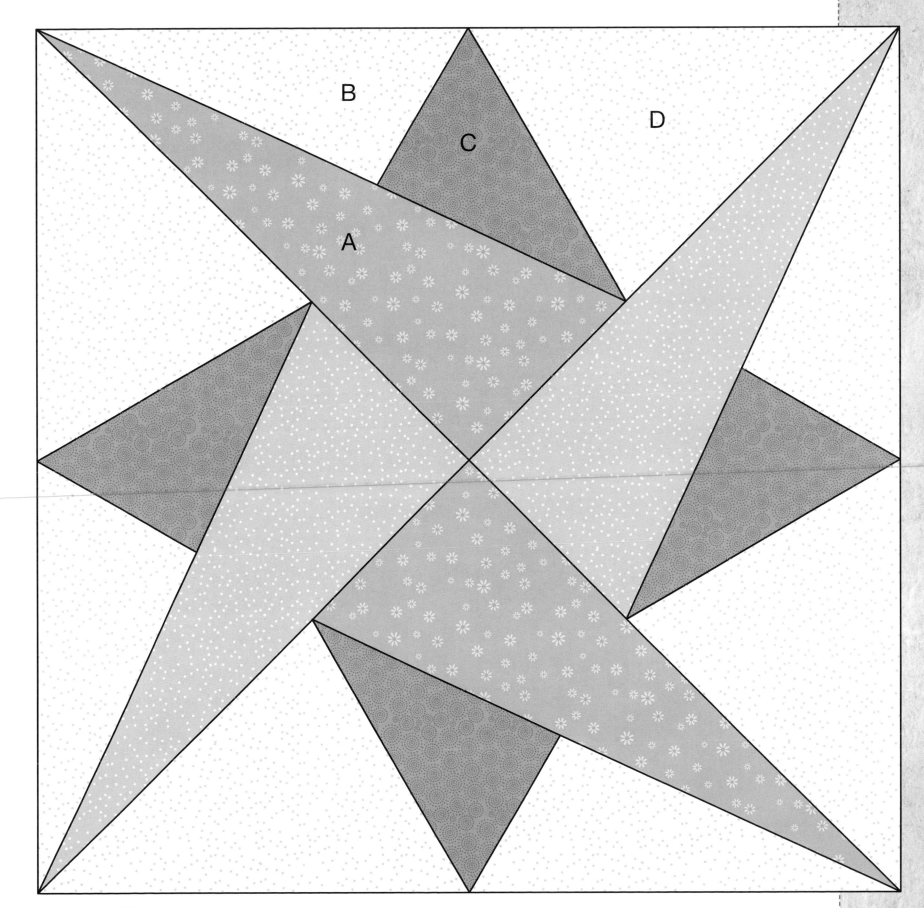

dimensional star full-size pattern

log cabin heart

Leslie McJunkin chose Log Cabin Heart for her block and embroidered words of encouragement on the finished piece. To see the entire quilt, turn to page 201.

Submitted by Sew-Ciety
Castle Rock, Colorado

assemble the block

1 Make center unit by sewing A to A, add BB, then CC, finally D.

2 Make EG unit; sew to center unit.

3 Make EF unit; sew to center and top.

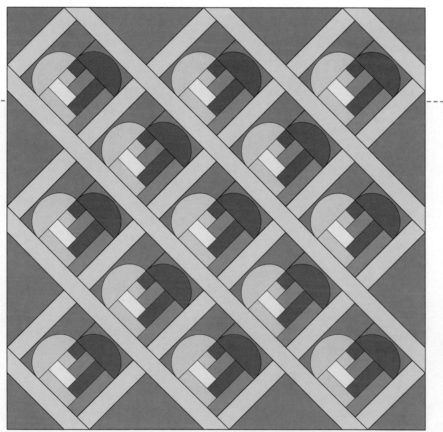

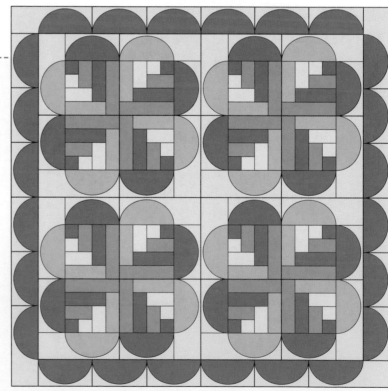

try this
Adding sashing diagonally forms a trellis effect on this pretty heart quilt.

look again
Scallops appear around the quilt edge when the top of the heart is used on the border. Rotating the blocks with the points to the center makes a flowerlike shape.

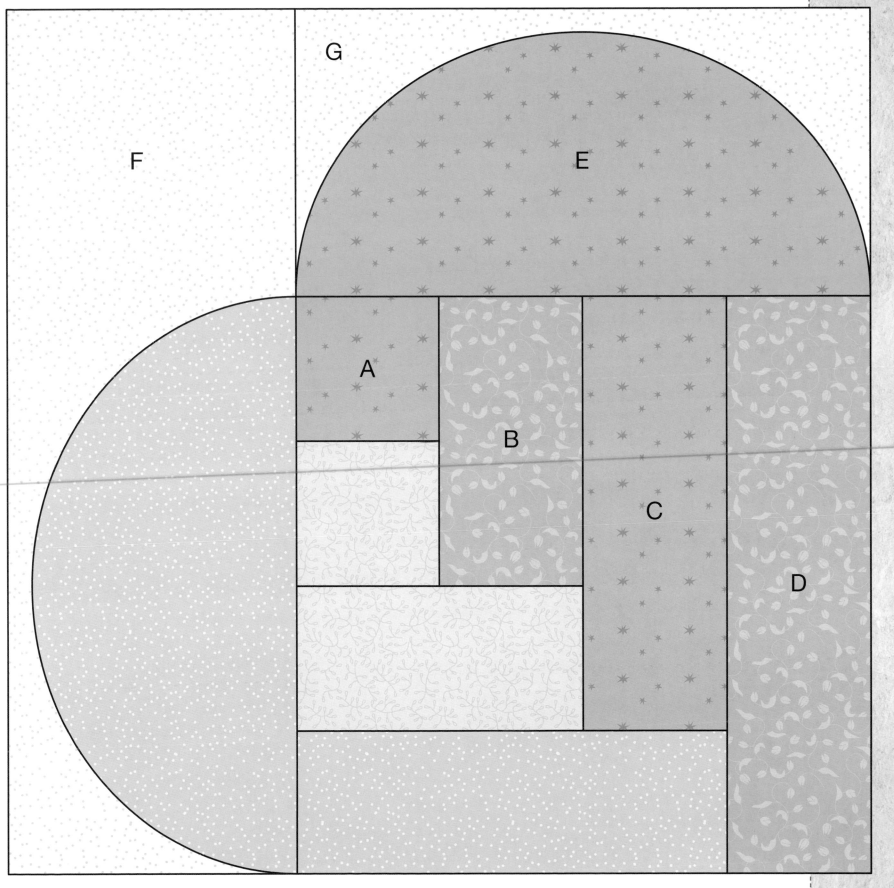

log cabin heart full-size pattern

windblown square

The women who come to this quilt shop also knit. Not to be outdone, the women who knit and crochet made a quilt to be auctioned and also turned in more than 30 pink-and-white chemo caps to the local Northwest Cancer Care Center. To see the entire quilt, turn to page 198.

Submitted by Quilt Lounge and Knittery
Deer Park, Washington

assemble the block

1 Make light and dark AA (16 times).
2 Make 4 rows of AA units, referring to pattern.
3 Sew rows together, placing rows as in pattern.

try this
When this two-color block is placed side by side an all-over design forms. The pieced quilt appears intricate and complicated but is actually very easy to piece.

look again
Using three or more colors in combinations that create secondary designs is another option for this versatile block.

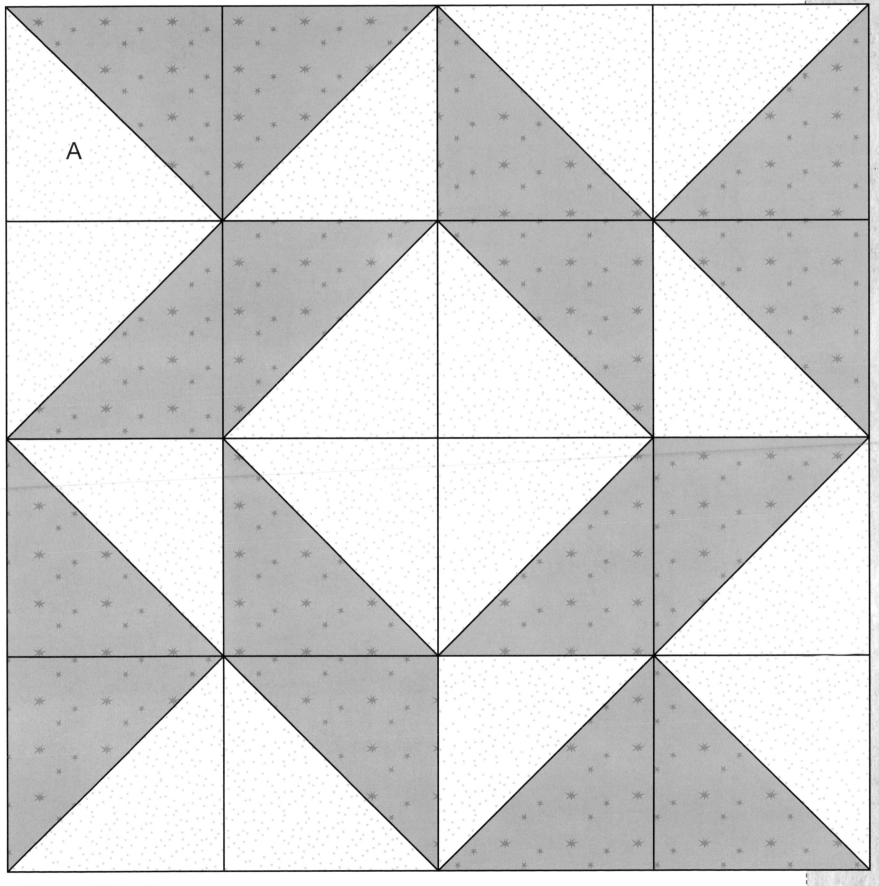

A

windblown square full-size pattern

triangle block

The women from the North Star Quilter's Guild created a tribute to the victims of breast cancer by using a simple block and pinks from the same palette. To see the entire quilt, turn to page 201.

Submitted by North Star Quilters Guild
Vancouver, Washington

assemble the block

1 Make AA unit (2 times).
2 Make AABB unit (2 times) for Rows 1 and 3.
3 Make BBB unit for Row 2.
4 Sew rows together to form block.

try this
Setting the blocks on point reveals a plaid appearance in this bold design.

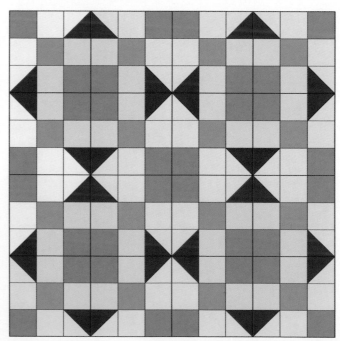

look again
Four large squares and diamonds appear in this arrangement of the Triangle Block.

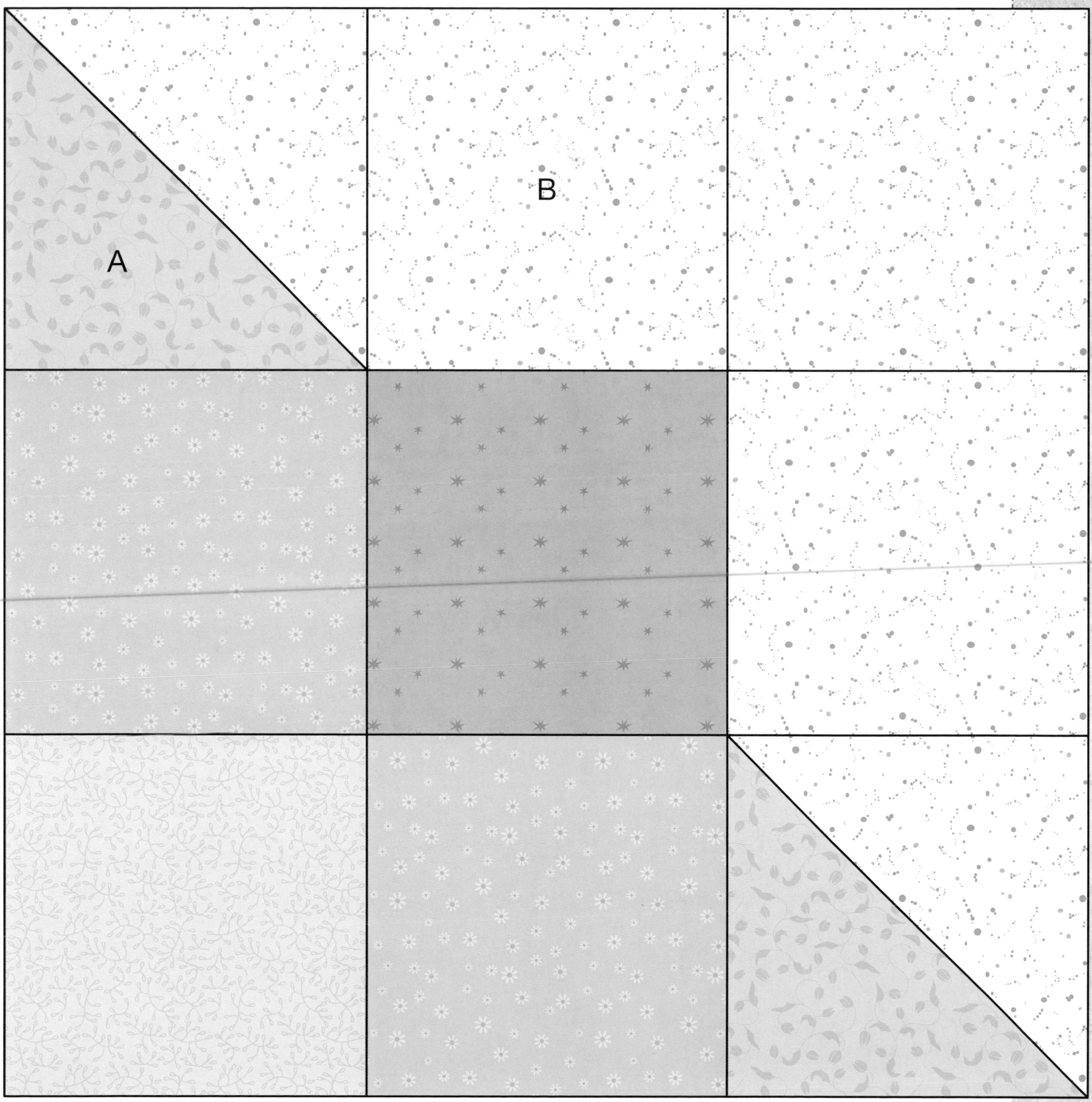

triangle block full-size pattern

A

B

diamond in a square

This active society of quilters from Mineola, New York, assembled 16 quilts for the cause. This block, from one of the sampler quilts, used bright pinks and neutrals. To see the entire quilt, turn to page 197.

*Submitted by Long Island Quilters Society
Mineola, New York*

assemble the block

1 Make AAAA unit (4 times).
2 Make BCBD unit (4 times).
3 Sew AAAABCBDAAAA (2 times) to make Rows 1 and 3.
4 Sew BCBDEDBCB for Row 2.
5 Sew Rows 1, 2, and 3 together.

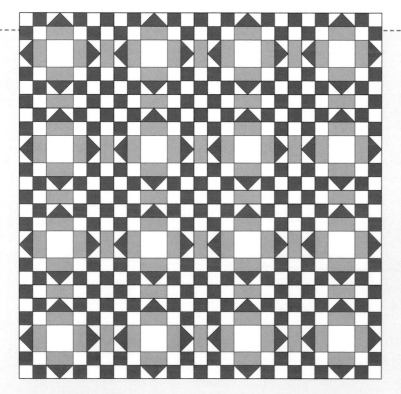

try this
Add sashing using the AADAA pieces between the blocks for a stunning look.

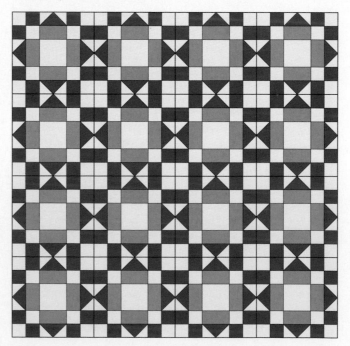

look again
Blocks set in straight rows resemble window panes with several interlocking shapes.

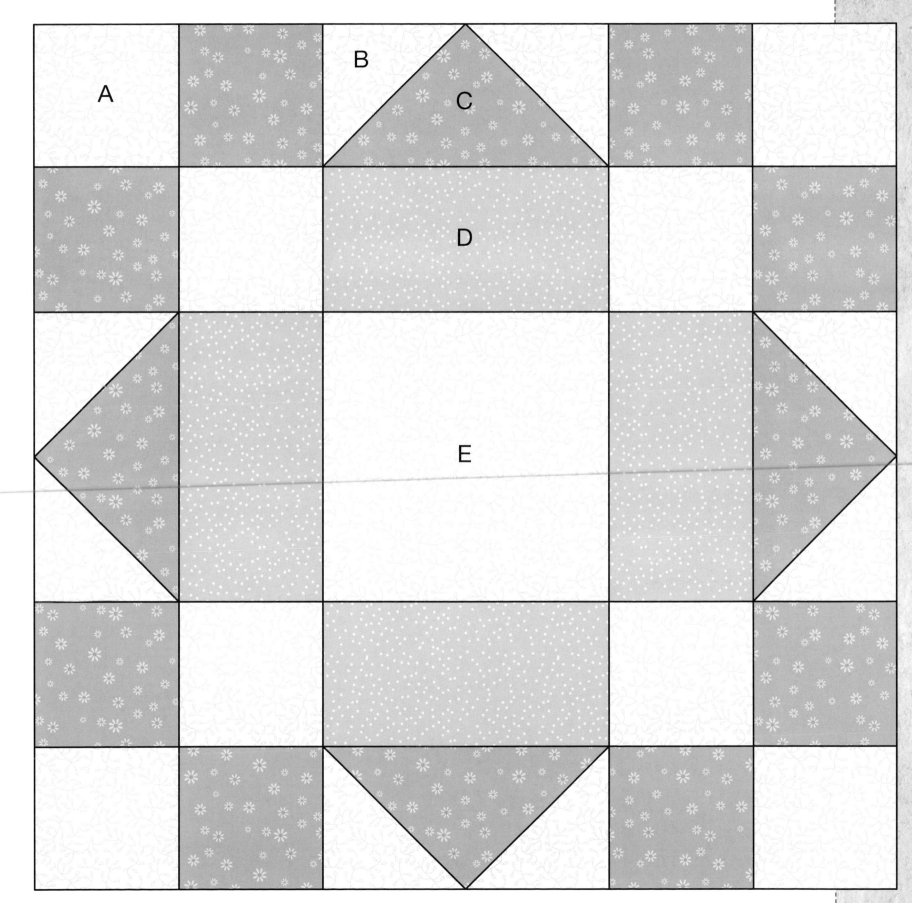

diamond in a square full-size pattern

heart petals

Bonnie Dank, who works on many charity projects, designed this appliqué block. Retired from the Army, Bonnie often works at Walter Reed Hospital, where she and quilting friends hold quilting seminars. To see the entire quilt, turn to page 197.

Submitted by And Sew It Goes Quilting Savage, Maryland

assemble the block

1 Appliqué leaves first to background A.

2 Appliqué the hearts next, slightly overlapping.

3 Appliqué center of flower last.

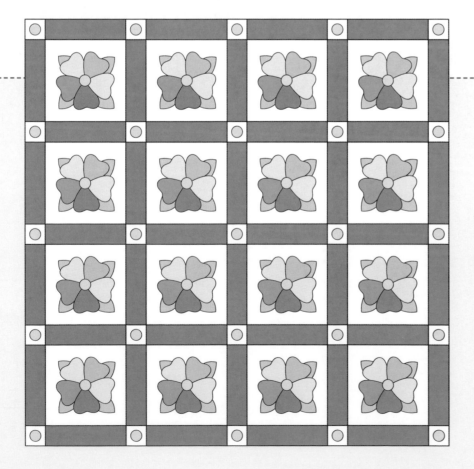

try this

For eye catching detail, appliqué the flower center on sashing squares between sashing strips.

A

heart petals full-size pattern

nosegay

JoNell Hester, her mother, and Mary Foster pieced this quilt in honor of friends Gaynell Stewart and Anna Lee Hawn. Fellow guild member Odell Nickerson hand-quilted it. JoNell writes, "I have been involved with four quilts and have been overwhelmed at the wonderful response to this cause." To see the entire quilt, turn to page 201.

Submitted by Rugby Quilters Guild
Hendersonville, Tennessee

assemble the block

1 Join C pieces into 4 rows.
2 Join rows to make a C square unit.
3 Make AA unit, ArAr unit, and BB unit.
4 Sew BB unit to ArAr and AA to C square unit; join sections.

try this
Placing the Nosegay block side by side creates waves of color and movement.

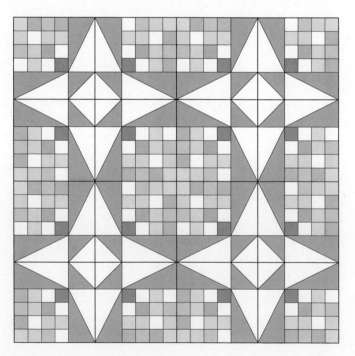

look again
Setting four Nosegay blocks corner to corner forms wide stars and checkerboards.

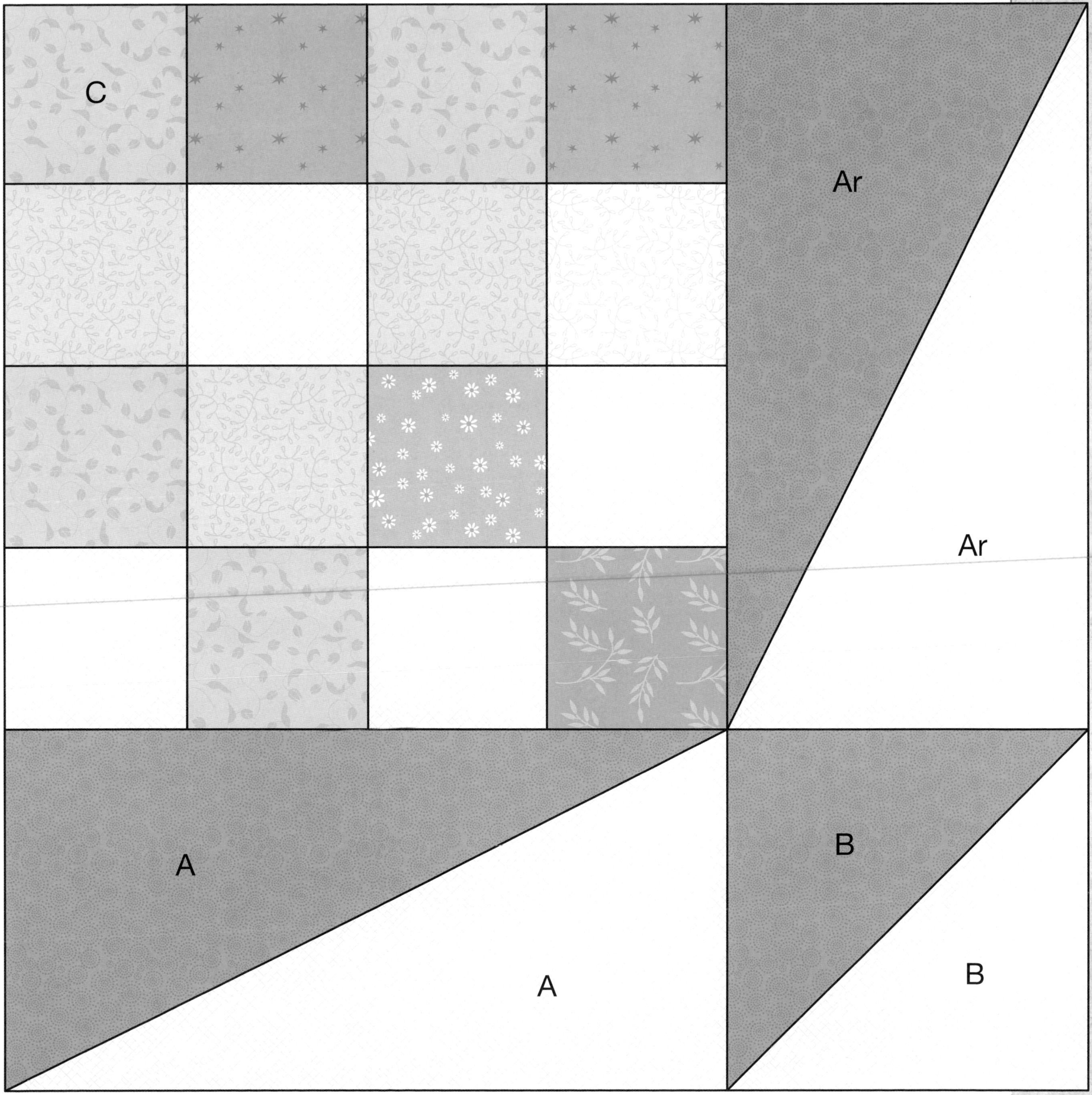

C

Ar

Ar

A

A

B

B

nosegay full-size pattern

drunkard's path

The Drunkard's Path block pattern is a favorite of Marlene Capehart, who pieced this quilt in honor of her cousin Carol Vida. This group of quilters, who call themselves The Quilting Angels, had so many blocks donated that they still had blocks remaining after making 20 quilts. To see the entire quilt, turn to page 202.

Submitted by Quilts by Eagle Mountain Products
Azle, Texas

assemble the block

1 Make AB unit (4 times).
2 Sew the AB units in rows.
3 Sew the rows together to make the block.

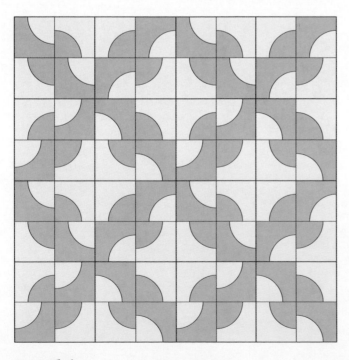

try this
This is the traditional layout for a Drunkard's Path block.

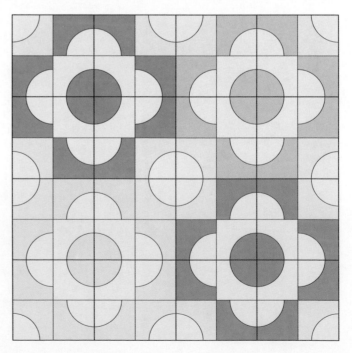

look again
By changing color placement and shifting units within each block, medallions and circles take shape.

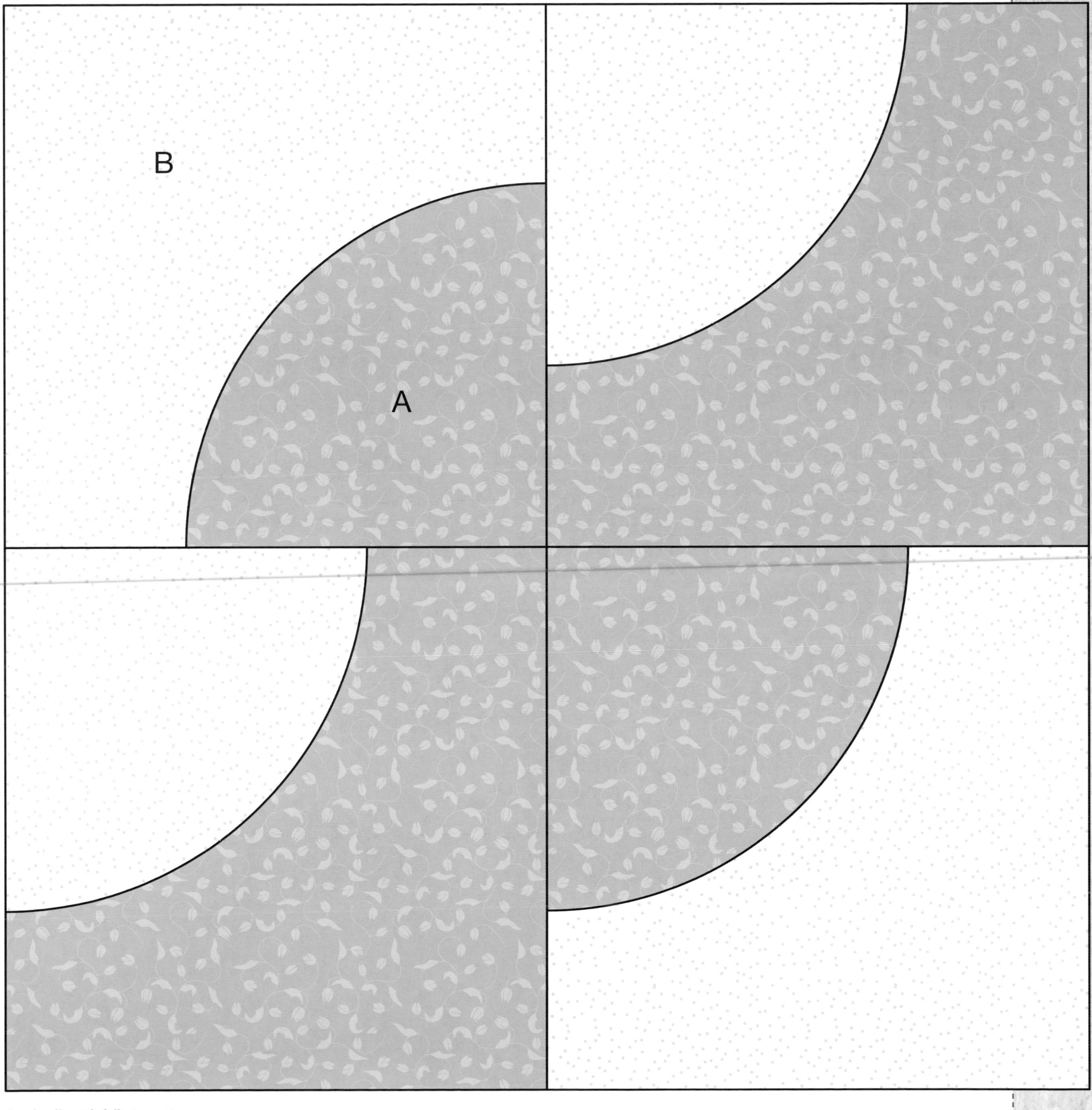

B

A

drunkard's path full-size pattern

welcome basket

This artistic block used a floral print cut to resemble a bouquet to fill the pieced basket. Place whatever you like in the basket block. To see the entire quilt turn to page 203.

Submitted by Flying Geese Fabrics
Albany, New York

assemble the block

1 Appliqué handle to C to make handle section.
2 Make BB unit (6 times).
3 Join in rows with a single B piece at the end of each row.
4 Join the rows, adding B piece to make pieced triangle.
5 Make AB and ArB units; add to pieced triangle to make basket section.
6 Sew the basket section to the handle section to complete the block.

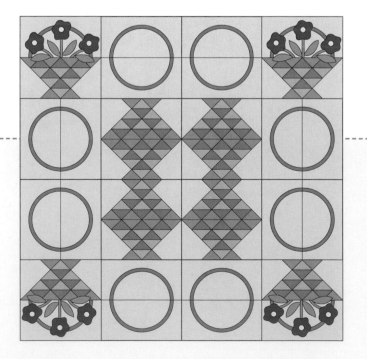

try this

Borrow the flowers from the Three Flowers block, page 190, for the corner blocks and use the handles and baskets from this block to make an unusual quilt.

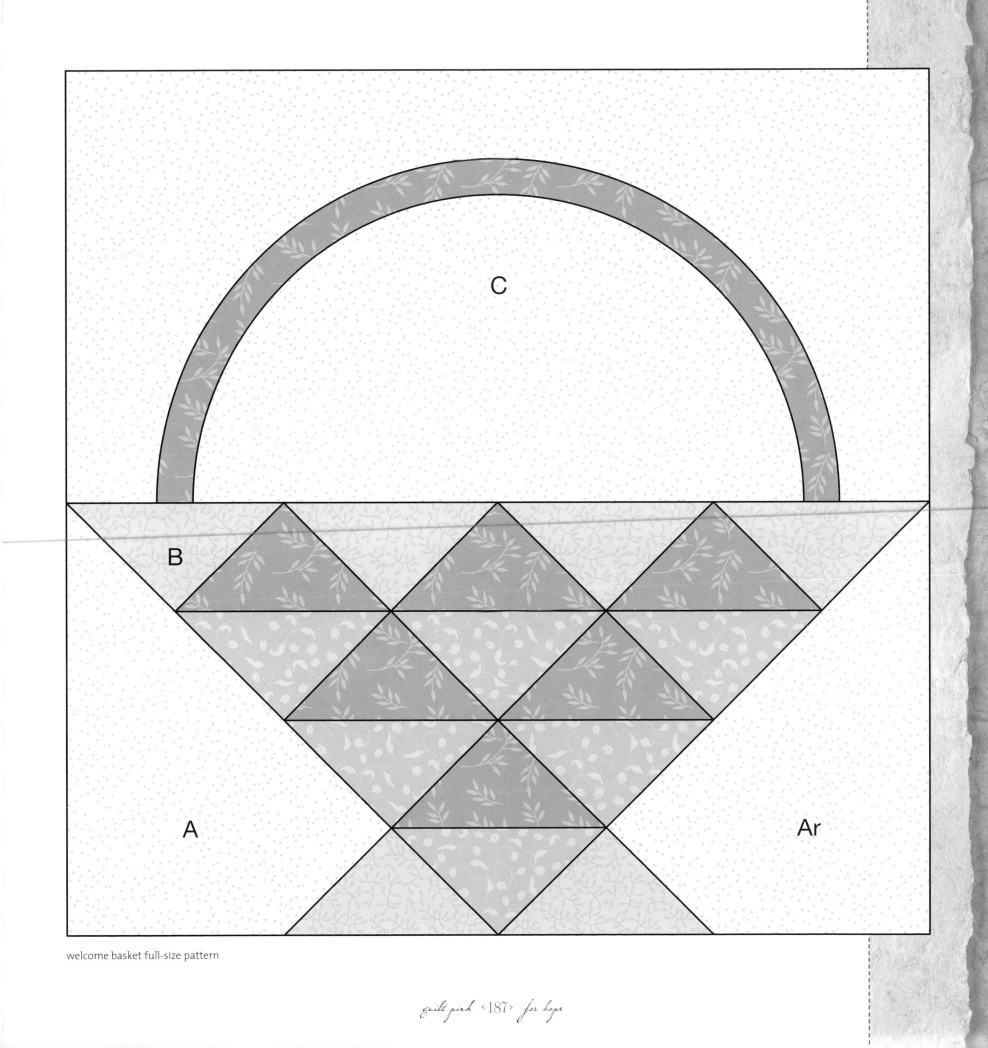

welcome basket full-size pattern

prairie queen

This delightful block was made by a group of quilters who call themselves The Wimpys, because as Jana Moser says, "We used to be able to quilt all night, but we can't anymore!" This quilt was made in honor of Judy Calvert, a quilting friend. To see the entire quilt, turn to page 202.

Submitted by Moser's Viking Center
Ellensburg, Washington

assemble the block

1 Make BB unit (4 times).

2 Make AAAA unit (4 times).

3 Sew BBAAAABB (2 times) for Rows 1 and 3.

4 Make AAAACAAAA unit for Row 2.

5 Sew rows together.

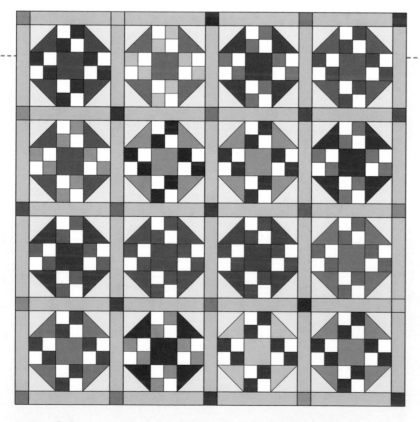

try this
Add sashing between blocks and choose strong colors for a colorful Prairie Queen quilt.

look again
With straight-set blocks, Four-Patch blocks become dominant.

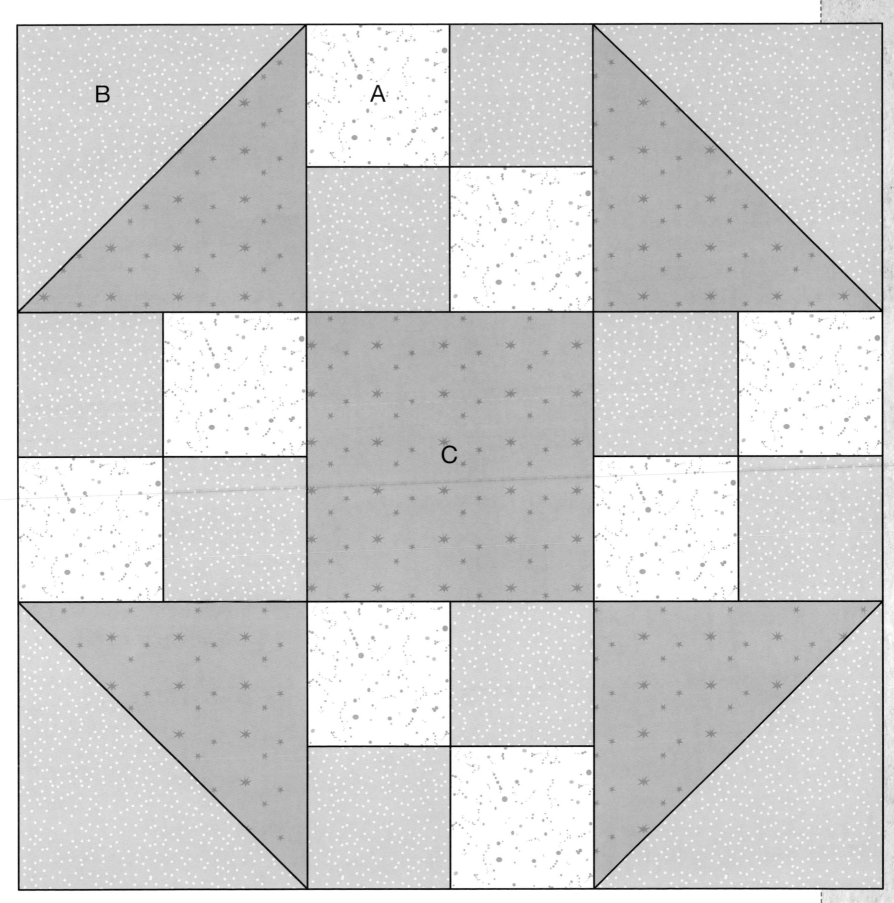

prairie queen full-size pattern

three flowers

Valerie Vincek designed this pretty block with appliquéd flowers. All the appliquéd blocks were made in honor of friends and family members who have been diagnosed with breast cancer. The name of each person is embroidered under each block. To see the entire quilt, turn to page 202.

Submitted by Calico and Cotton
Ocean City, New Jersey

assemble the block

1 Appliqué leaves first, then stems to background A.
2 Add flowers and basket next.
3 Add flower centers.

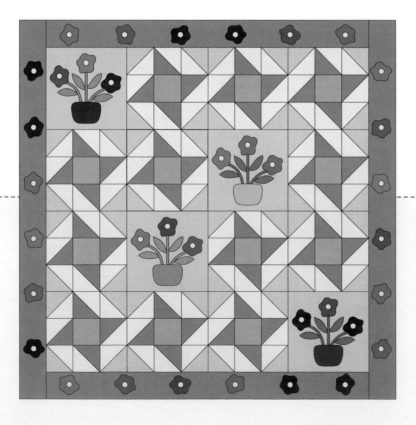

try this

Combine Friendship Star, page 130, with Three Flowers in an asymetrical design. Add a border of appliquéd flower shapes taken from the main block for a striking effect.

A

three flowers full-size pattern

signature block

This block was designed to be part of a signature quilt. The blocks are simple to make even for a beginning quilter. The simplicity of the block allows for each quilter to honor or memorialize a loved one. To see the entire quilt, turn to page 202.

Submitted by Sisters' Scraps Quilt Shop
Amarillo, Texas

assemble the block

1 Make BBB unit.

2 Add A to each side to complete the block.

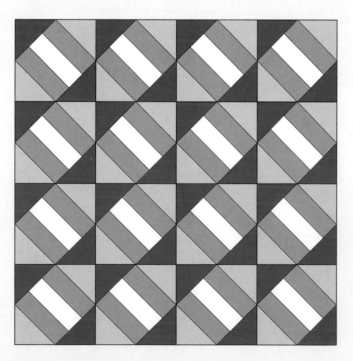

look again
Placed side by side, the signatures can be embroidered at a consistent angle.

try this
Lay out the blocks by rotating the position back and forth to create a crisscross effect.

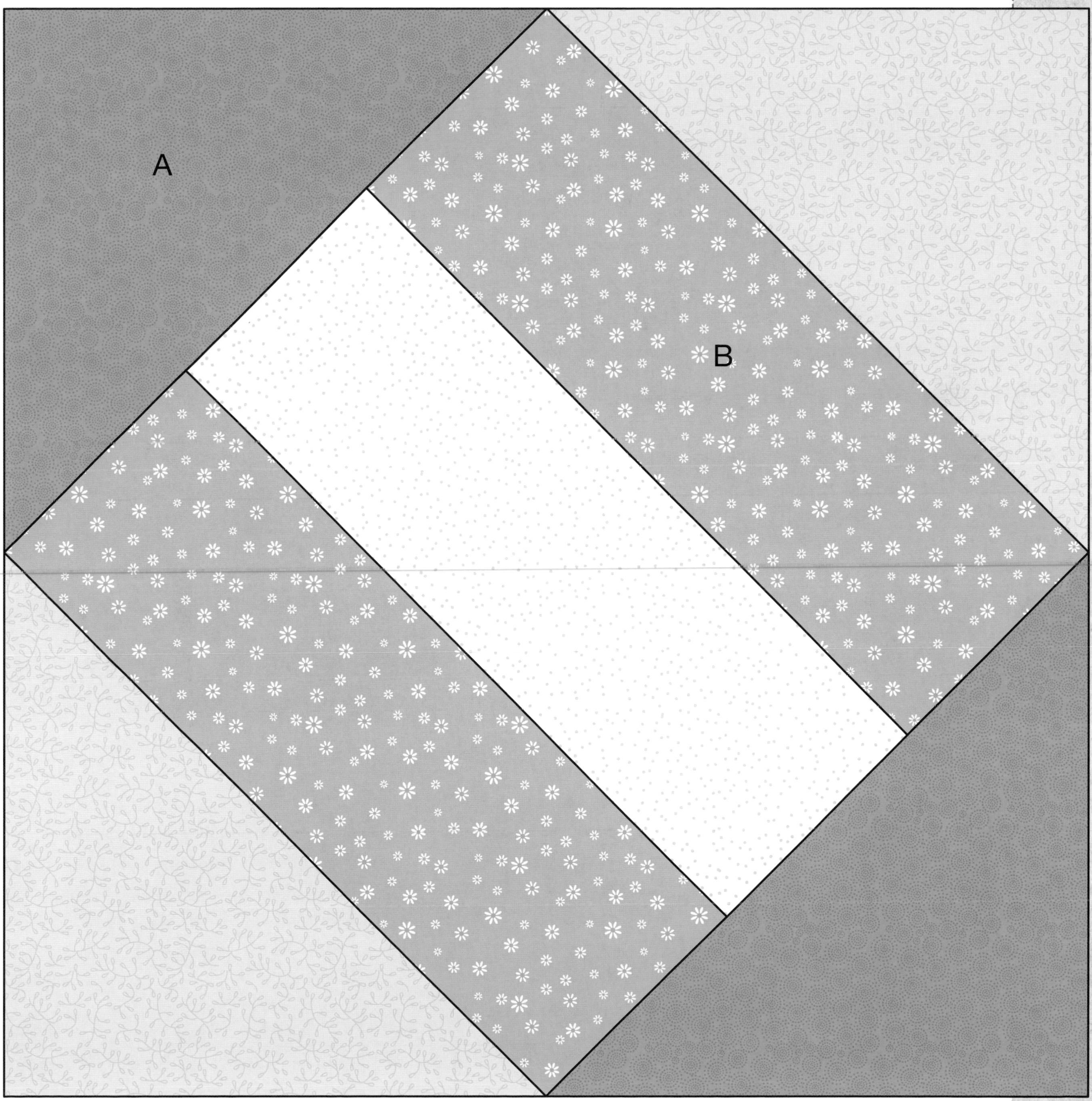

A

B

signature block full-size pattern

Quilt Gallery

The quilts in this section, donated by quilters across the country, feature some of the blocks shown on pages 92 to 193.

1 Block patterns and instructions for some blocks are shown on pages 94, 104, 112, and 126.

2 Block pattern and instructions on page 96. Quilt by Terry Atkinson.

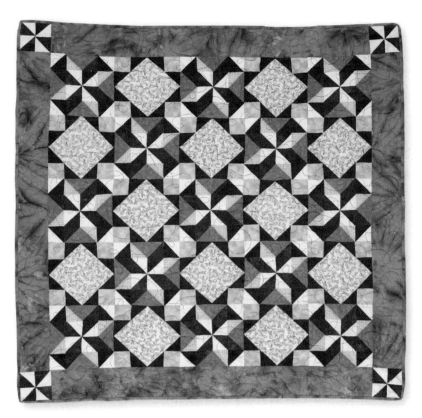

3 Block patterns and instructions on pages 98 and 116.

4 Block pattern and instructions on page 100.

5 Block pattern and instructions on page 102. Quilt by Lois Logsdon, Country Crossroads Quilter, Warm Wrappings Group

6 Block patterns and instructions for some blocks are shown on pages 106 and 148.

7 Block patterns and instructions for some blocks
  are shown on pages 108, 138, and 160.

8 Block pattern and instructions on page 110.

9 Block pattern and instructions on page 114.

10 Block pattern and instructions on page 118.

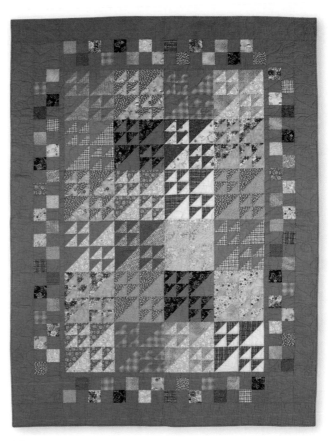

11 Block patterns and instructions for some blocks are shown on pages 120 and 180.

12 Block pattern and instructions on page 122.

13 Block patterns and instructions for some blocks are shown on pages 124 and 178.

14 Block patterns and instructions for some blocks as shown on pages 128, 140 and 170.

15 Block pattern and instructions on page 130.

16 Block pattern and instructions for one block on page 132.

17 Block pattern and instructions for one block on page 134.

18 Block pattern and instructions for some blocks are shown on pages 136, 150, and 174.

19 Block pattern and instructions for some blocks are shown on pages 142, 158, and 166.

20 Block pattern and instructions on page 144.

21 Block pattern and instructions on page 146.

22 Block pattern and instructions on page 152.

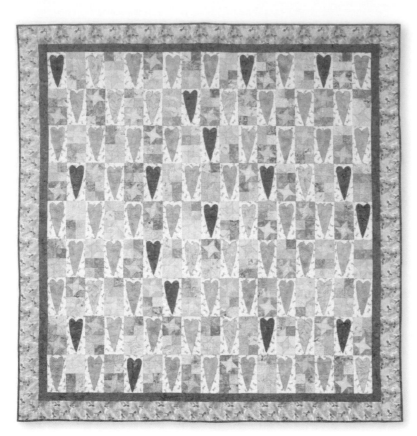

23 Block pattern and instructions on page 154.
   Quilt by Debbie Mumm.

24 Block pattern and instructions for one block on page 156.

25 Block pattern and instructions for one block on page 162.

26 Block pattern and instructions on page 164.

27 Block pattern and instructions for one block on page 168.

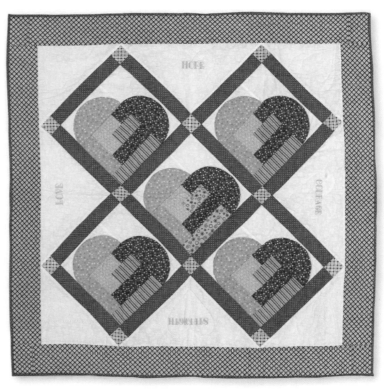

28 Block pattern and instructions on page 172. Quilt Design by Eleanor Burns, *Still Stripping After 25 years.*

29 Block pattern and instructions on page 176.

30 Block pattern and instructions on page 182.

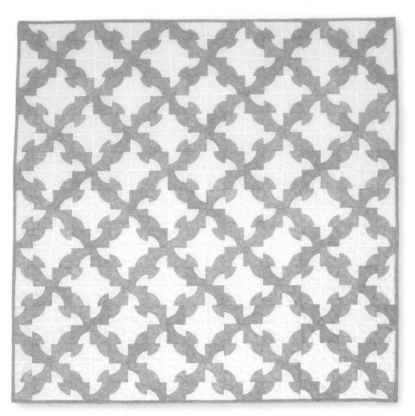

31 Block pattern and instructions on page 184.

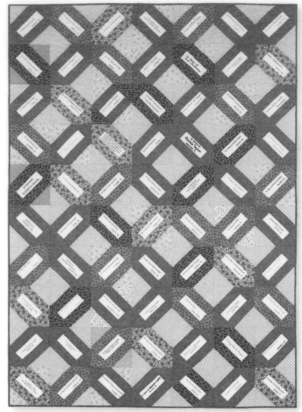

32 Block pattern and instructions on page 192.
Quilt by Kris Kerrigan.

33 Block pattern and instructions on page 188.

34 Block pattern and instructions for one block
on page 190.

35 Block pattern and instructions for one block on page 186.

Quilts Submitted by:

1 Quilters Unlimited,
   Mt. Vernon Chapter
   Alexandria, Virginia
2 Hingeley Road Quilt Shop
   Floodwood, Minnesota
3 Quilters Workshop
   Oak Harbor, Washington
4 Minnesota Quilters Inc.
   Minneapolis, Minnesota
5 R Lily Stem Quilts
   Modesto, California
6 Country Quiltworks
   Montgomeryville, Pennsylvania
7 Calico, Canvas & Colors
   Racine, Wisconsin
8 Calico Hutch
   Hayward, Minnesota
9 Debbie's Quilt Shop
   Paradise, California

10 Quilted Treasures
   Rogers, Minnesota
11 And Sew It Goes
   Savage, Maryland
12 Eagle Creek Quilt Shop
   Shakopee, Minnesota
13 Long Island Quilters Society
   Mineola, New York
14 A Quilter's Heart
   Grimsby, Ontario, Canada
15 Just Friends Quilt Guild
   Colo, Iowa
16 Fabric Boutique Quilt Shop
   Las Vegas, Nevada
17 Georgia's Quilting
   Obsession
   Beaumont, California
18 Quilt Lounge and Knittery
   Deer Park, Washington

19 In Stitches Quilt Shop
   Rushville, Indiana
20 Stitch 'N Time
   Jackson, Wyoming
21 Walcott Sewing & Vacuum
   Madison, Wisconsin
22 Timeless Treasures
   McGregor, Minnesota
23 Fabric Corner
   Topeka, Kansas
24 The Quilt Shop & Vac 'N Sew
   Conway, New Hampshire
25 Cotton Fields Quilt & Knit
   Avondale, Arizona
26 Stitcher's Crossing
   Madison, Wisconsin
27 The Quilt Shop & Vac 'N Sew
   Conway, New Hampshire

28 Sew-Ciety
   Castle Rock, Colorado
29 North Star Quilters Guild
   Vancouver, Washington
30 Rugby Quilters Guild
   Hendersonville, Tennessee
31 Quilts by Eagle Mountain
   Products
   Azle, Texas
32 Sisters' Scraps Quilt Shop
   Amarillo, Texas
33 Moser's Viking Center
   Ellensburg, Washington
34 Calico & Cotton
   Ocean City, New Jersey
35 Flying Geese Fabrics
   Albany, New York

Quilt Basics

fabrics, tools & supplies

Before beginning a quilt project, in your work area assemble all the fabric, tools, and supplies you'll be using. Experienced stitchers may have all the necessary equipment and some specialized tools; novice and beginning sewers will learn along the way which tools make cutting, sewing, piecing, and finishing easier and more pleasant. New and improved tools and supplies, adapted especially for quilting, are regularly introduced in quilting and fabric stores and in quiltmaking and sewing classes.

fabrics

One-hundred-percent cotton fabric remains the best choice for quiltmaking. Cotton minimizes seam distortion, presses crisply, and has a nice finish for hand and machine quilting. Project yardage requirements often specify 42- or 44/45-inch-wide fabrics, which are common in the industry. After removing the selvages from the fabric, the width is closer to 42 inches.

Prewashing fabrics is recommended. Prewashing fabrics offers quilters certainty as its main advantage. Although fabrics manufactured today resist bleeding and shrinkage, some of both occur in some fabrics, which is an unpleasant prospect for finished quilts. Prewashing fabrics prevents shrinkage and puckering in finished quilts, prevents dyes from running in finished quilts, removes excess sizing, and removes dust collected during shipping, handling, and storage. Prewashing also softens fabric for handling, and some quilters believe it is easier to quilt.

To prewash fabric, unfold it to a single layer, washing only like colors together, and allowing the fabric ample room in the washer. Place fabric pieces that measure less than ½ yard in zippered pillowcases or mesh bags to prevent them from tangling and twisting in the washer. Wash the fabric in warm water on delicate cycle. If the dyes from the fabric run, rinse the fabric until the water is clear.

Or, use a product that traps excess dyes in the prewash to prevent color transfer from one fabric to another. Do not use fabrics that have not stopped running or bleeding in quilts. Do not use fabric softener in the final rinse of the fabrics. Hang the fabric to dry, or tumble it in the dryer until just slightly damp. Steam-press the fabric before measuring, marking, and cutting.

If you choose not to prewash fabrics, the following will be helpful. Some quilters prefer piecing crisp, unwashed fabrics. When quilts are made with fabrics that have the same fiber content and thread count throughout, the fabrics will likely shrink uniformly with the first washing, giving the quilt a slightly puckered and antique look, which some quilters like. Also, for quilted projects that will never be laundered, such as wall hangings that can be vacuumed or shaken to remove the dust, prewashing may seem unnecessary; although a spill on the finished project may cause shrinkage and puckering or cause dyes to run. Using lighter-color fabrics eliminates the fear of color running, if not the issue of shrinkage. To test fabric to determine whether to prewash or not, cut two identical size and shape pieces from each fabric, including selvage edges. Soak one of each piece in water for several hours. Rinse the fabric until the water runs clear, lay it to dry, and press it smooth. Compare the fabric pieces for shrinkage and color.

batting

◆ Thin, cotton batting is a good choice for small or beginning projects because it adheres to fabric, requires less basting, and is easy to stitch through. Follow the stitch density (the distance between rows of quilting stitches that prevents the batting from shifting and bunching) for each batting type. Recommendations for stitch density are printed on packaging and are available at stores that sell batting by the yard. Cotton batting, a good choice for garments, conforms well to the body.

◆ Polyester batting is lightweight and inexpensive. In general, it springs back to its original height when compressed and adds puffiness to quilts. As it is quilted it tends to "beard" (work out between the weave of the fabric) more than natural fibers. Polyester fleece is denser and works well for quilting pillow tops and place mats.

◆ Wool batting is warm, has loft retention, and absorbs moisture, making it ideal for cool, damp climates. Wool batting also provides a flatter, natural, or antique look to quilts. Some wool batts require special care; read packaging labels carefully or check with sales people at quilting stores before purchasing wool batting for quilt projects.

tools & supplies

Table or other large, stable work surface: The work surface should be a comfortable height for reaching and cutting the fabric. A table, portable or stationary, adjacent to a sewing machine or quilting hoop is also useful for supporting the weight of the quilt while machine- or hand-quilting.

Cutting mat, acrylic ruler, and rotary cutter: These tools, which have revolutionized quilting, allow for several fabric layers to be cut accurately and easily. The fabric is laid on the mat, the ruler is held firmly on the fabric in position for cutting, and the sharp wheel like blade of the rotary cutter is rolled along the edge of the ruler to make straight cuts.

A self-healing cutting mat provides a surface for the cutting blade and prevents fabric from shifting as it is being cut. To allow for adjusting, layering, and cutting fabric, the recommended mat minimum size is 24×36 inches, with 1-inch grids marked along the surface. Place the cutting mat on a firm surface at approximately table or counter height.

Acrylic rulers vary in sizes and shapes, from small to large rectangles, squares, and triangles. For a basic ruler, choose a 6×24-inch ruler that has $\frac{1}{8}$-inch markings and a 45-degree angle marking. Some rulers have 30- and 60-degree angle markings as well as specialized angles for cutting triangles and other shapes.

Several styles of rotary cutters and replaceable cutting blades are available. Quilters usually find the style that best fits their grip. Additionally, some rotary cutters have blades for cutting more than straight cuts.

Scissors: Designate a sharp pair for cutting fabric only. Designate a pair for general purpose to cut paper, plastic, and template material. Also, small nippers or embroidery scissors are useful for clipping into seam allowances, clipping threads, and precisely cutting small irregular shapes.

Pins and pincushion or pinholder: Select good-quality, rustproof, long quilter's pins that have round heads for easy visibility and grasping. Use a stuffed pincushion or magnetic pinholder (if you don't have a computerized sewing machine) that you can transport between your cutting, sewing, and pressing areas.

Marking tools: Marking fabrics with specially made markers for sewing and quilting ensures that the marks will be removable when the project is finished. Depending on fabric content and color, look for chalks, pencils, and water- and air-soluble markers with the quilting supplies at fabric and quilt stores. Test marking tools on fabric scraps before using on your quilt.

Template plastic: Use this material to trace and cut fabric shapes that cannot be cut using an acrylic ruler and rotary cutter or as an option to using a rotary cutter and acrylic ruler. The material comes in sheets about $\frac{1}{16}$ inch thick and appears slightly frosted. Use general purpose scissors to cut the material.

Quilt Basics continued

Sewing machine: Use a clean sewing machine that is in good working order, sews reliably straight stitches, and has even tension. Have a supply of sewing machine needles that fit the machine, and change the needle regularly to ensure good stitches and prevent needle breakage during sewing. A nice added feature is a ¼-inch sewing foot for sewing precise seam allowances; an alternative is marking the needle plate with masking tape at the precise ¼-inch width between the stitched seam and the raw edge of the fabric. Wind several bobbins with thread before beginning each project to have them ready when you need them.

Walking foot: This sewing machine accessory frees the feed dogs to allow the backing, batting, and quilt top layers to remain smooth and even rather than bunching while machine-quilting.

Darning foot, hopper foot, or free-motion foot: This sewing machine accessory is used for free-motion stitching through single or layered fabrics. Some machines are equipped with this accessory; to purchase one for your machine, have available the machine brand and model.

Threads: For hand- or machine-piecing, use 100-percent-cotton or cotton-covered polyester thread. For hand quilting, use 100-percent-cotton or cotton-covered polyester quilting thread, which is stronger than hand- or machine-sewing threads. For machine quilting, use 100-percent-cotton or cotton-covered polyester quilting thread, fine nylon thread, or threads specifically made for machine quilting.

Hand-sewing needles: The needles used for piecing, appliquéing, and quilting are sharps and betweens; the larger the number, the finer the needle. Betweens are short with a narrow eye to sew through fabric layers without leaving marks. Common needle sizes are #11 and #12 sharps for hand sewing and appliqué, and sizes #8, #9, and #10 betweens for hand quilting, with #9 suggested for beginning quilters. Often quilters like to sew with fine needles to obtain tiny stitches and larger needles for obvious stitches.

Thimbles: Use metal, plastic, or leather thimbles, or adhesive strips on fingertips to help push the needle through fabric, relieving some of the pressure and preventing skin punctures. The wide variety of sizes, styles, and materials allows for selecting thimbles for multiple purposes.

Safety pins: Use brass or nickel-coated, rust proof safety pins to temporarily hold together fabrics, to hold together the quilt layers for basting, or to use instead of basting threads for machine quilting. Size 1 is a common size to use with sewing. To pin-baste a large quilt for machine quilting, use between 350 to 500 Size 1 safety pins placed approximately 6 inches apart; remove the pins as you quilt.

Iron and ironing board: A good quality steam iron and a sturdy ironing board or pressing table are important for pressing throughout the piecing process to ensure accurate piecing and finished size of units, blocks, rows, and the quilt top. Press along each step of the way whether hand-sewing or machine-sewing. When pressing, lay the hot iron on the fabric, press firmly, and lift. Avoid sliding or pushing the iron across the fabric, which distorts seams and shapes, affecting the finished project.

Fusible-adhesive material: Available packaged and by the yard, this fusible adhesive is bonded to the wrong side of fabric for fusing two layers of fabric together. The adhesive has a paper side for drawing or tracing shapes and stabilizing the fabric for cutting. After cutting out the shape, the paper is removed, and the adhesive side is pressed to the right side of another fabric. The edges of the fabric shape can be hand- or machine-stitched, left unfinished, or finished with other techniques.

Freezer paper: Press the waxed side of this slightly stiff paper to the wrong side of fabric as an option to needle-turning the raw edges of fabric shapes that may distort during stitching, or use it as an alternative to stiff adhesive-backed material. Freezer paper can be cut to shape, minus seam allowances, and pressed to the wrong side of fabric. Cut fabric beyond the freeze-paper shape for a seam allowance, then turn and press under the fabric edges toward the freezer paper. Pin or baste the shaped piece in place, appliqué most of the shape, insert the needle between the appliqué and foundation fabric to loosen the freezer paper from the shape, pull out the paper, and finish stitching the shape in place. Freezer paper also can be used as a stabilizer for writing on fabric, such as making labels to sew to a finished quilt or for signing fabric to make into a signature or album quilt.

Quilting frame or hoop: A variety of sizes and shapes of frames, from room-size to portable handheld sizes, support the size, weight, and layers of the quilt. Stretching the sandwiched quilt top, batting, and backing in a frame or hoop before quilting creates tension and a firm surface in order to take small, even stitches by hand, and allows freedom for working with both hands. Quilting hoops, made of wood or sturdy plastic, are deeper than embroidery hoops to accommodate the quilt layers. A portable handheld or tabletop 14-inch to 18-inch circular wooden hoop is adequate for quilting even a large quilt.

select a first project

Choosing a project is the first step in successful quilting, whether you're new to quilting or have quilted for years. With the array of fabrics, projects, patterns, books, and ideas available, settling on one project to see through to completion may seem daunting. If you need help, follow these tips:

Find a friendly place. A quilt supply store or fabric store where employees are knowledgeable about quilting is a good place to start. Often the staff at quilting stores are quilters and eager to share their knowledge and excitement about the craft.

Start small. Making a wall hanging, table runner, pillow cover, or baby quilt that takes less time than a full-size quilt allows you to experience success and look forward to a new project.

Take classes. Quilting shops and fabric stores offer a variety of classes—from beginner to advanced—and offer timesaving tips along the way. Taking classes with peers allows you to benefit from one another's experiences and share your excitement for all the little successes.

Purchase kits. Sometimes selecting all the fabrics for a project seems daunting. By purchasing a kit that contains pattern, fabrics, and instructions, a major hurdle is already accomplished, and you can get started sooner.

Be square. Projects that are made by piecing squares, right triangles, and rectangles are easier for beginners than piecing odd shapes and angles. Appliquéing shapes, as long as the technique is kept simple, also is a good beginning project.

Love it. Encourage yourself to finish each project by choosing designs and fabrics that you're eager to finish, share, show off, and use.

machine piecing

Cut the pattern pieces from fabric, including seam allowances. Place two cut pieces of fabric, right sides together, aligning raw edges, and pin them together. Place the layered pieces under the presser foot of the sewing machine, lower the needle, and sew an exact ¼-inch seam allowance to join pieces of the unit.

Quilt Basics continued

To chain-piece several units without breaking the thread between each unit, pin together and feed another unit right behind the finished unit, and begin stitching. After chaining several units, raise the presser foot, and clip the threads between each unit. Press the seam allowances of each unit, using an up and down motion with the iron rather than a sliding motion to avoid distorting the seams.

hand piecing

Mark pattern pieces on wrong side of fabric, drawing around the finished size of the patterns and allowing space between pattern pieces to draw and/or cut ¼-inch seam allowances. Draw a ¼-inch seam allowance around each pattern piece, or cut out the pieces gauging a ¼-inch seam allowance by eye. Pin together pattern pieces, right sides together, aligning pieces along the drawn finished line, which is the sewing line.

Insert a threaded needle at the seam line; backstitch to lock the stitch in place. Hand-sew the pieces together, weaving the needle in and out to take 4 to 6 stitches at a time and sewing 8 to 10 stitches per inch. Back-stitch and end the last stitch with a loop knot; cut the thread. Press the seams to one side.

appliqué

If you're a beginner, select an appliqué design with straight lines and gentle curves. Learning to make sharp points and tiny stitches takes practice. Some appliquéd motifs are pieced then appliquéd. The project instructions may suggest marking the position of each piece on a foundation block before cutting and piecing the design.

Basic hand-appliqué method: Pin and baste appliqué shapes to foundation fabrics, overlapping multiple pieces if required, following position markings on illustrations, and referring to photographs. For hidden stitching, appliqué the shapes in place using matching thread and small stitches, using a hand-quilting needle or a long milliner's needle to catch a few threads of the folded edge of the shape and a few threads of the foundation fabric. Use the point of the needle to work the fabric, tucking in the seam allowance and adjusting points and V-shapes of the appliqué. Finish stitching by taking an extra slipstitch at the end of the appliqué shape; carry the needle and thread to the inside of the shape or the underside of the foundation fabric, and clip the thread close to the fabric. A short tail of thread will remain hidden in a seam or behind the appliqué. When appliquéing lightweight fabrics and the foundation fabric shows through the appliqué, carefully cut away the foundation fabric behind the appliqué to within ¼ inch of the hand stitching.

For decorative appliqué stitches, use heavier-weight and contrasting-color threads, allowing the project size and motif to guide the thread selection.

Machine-hemstitch appliqué method: Sewing machines that have a setting or attachment for hem-stitching or blind-stitching can be used to appliqué shapes to foundation fabrics. Use the freezer paper method, page 209, to prepare the appliqué shape for stitching, and follow the instructions with your sewing machine for setting the stitch length and width to appliqué.

Fusible adhesive method: To fuse fabric shapes to foundation fabric without turning under a seam allowance, apply fusible adhesive to the appliqué fabric, trace and cut out a shape on the paper side of the fusible adhesive, remove the paper, and fuse the shape to the foundation fabric. Finish the appliqué by hand or machine, leave it unfinished, or use fabric glue to finish the edges.

To fuse large appliqué shapes to foundation fabric and eliminate the stiffness of the fusible adhesive, trace and cut out the design ¼ to ½ inch along the outer edge of the design. Fuse only the outline of the design to the appliqué fabric, then to the foundation fabric. The piece will be secure enough to finish stitching without the stiffness or bulk of the adhesive.

Freezer paper method: To turn neat seam allowances on appliqué shapes for hand or machine appliqué, trace the pattern shapes on freezer paper. Press the waxed side of the paper to the wrong side of the fabric. Turn under and press the seam allowance along the paper edge, clipping and trimming tight inner and outer corners and working them neatly to the underside with a needle or quilting pin. For hand appliqué, baste the shape to the foundation fabric and stitch in place until a small section remains unstitched. Insert the needle in the opening, loosen the freezer paper, remove it, and finish stitching. For machine appliqué, press the freezer-paper lined shape from the front and back side to set the seams. Remove the freezer paper, hand-baste the seam allowance in place, trimming and clipping as needed for the shape to lie flat. Position the appliqué shape on the foundation fabric and stitch in place. Remove the basting stitches.

Needle-turn method: Freezer paper in the shape of the appliqué can be fused to the back of the fabric first to help in turning under crisp edges. Cut out the appliqué shape ⅛ inch beyond the finished design. Baste or pin the shape to a foundation fabric. Use matching thread and a small needle to turn under the seam allowance and blind-stitch along the edge of the shape.

Double-appliqué method: To ease the challenge of turning curved edges, face the appliqué shape before sewing it to foundation fabric. Trace an appliqué shape on fabric; cut out the shape, allowing a ¼-inch seam allowance. Place the shape facedown on a piece of sheer nonwoven interfacing. Sew around the shape for a ¼-inch seam allowance; grade the seams and clip the curves. Make a small clip in the center of the interfacing and turn the appliqué shape to the right side through the opening. Press the shape from the right side, rolling under the seam line toward the interfacing side. Stitch the appliqué shape to the foundation fabric.

Making bias stems and vines: For singlefold bias strips, cut fabric on the bias approximately twice the finished width and slightly longer than required. If necessary, piece together bias strips for long vines. With the wrong side of the strip facing up, press the long raw edges toward the center of the strip. Pin or baste the bias strips to the foundation fabric and appliqué in place.

For doublefold bias strips, cut strips approximately two and one-half the finished width. Fold the strip in half wrong sides together; sew a ⅛- to ¼-inch seam along the raw edges. Press the seam and raw edges to finish under the fold. Pin, baste, and appliqué the strip to the foundation fabric. For making bias strips easier, bias bar sewing tools are available.

machine paper piecing

This method of machine piecing allows for sewing small pieces of fabric into intricate designs because the fabrics are stabilized by the paper or fabric foundation. A block design is traced onto lightweight paper or other purchased stabilizer; fabric pieces are then sewn to the underside of the design in numerical order. Sewing the fabrics to the underside creates an identical design to be traced rather than a mirror image, which would be created by sewing fabrics to the traced side of the design. Sew the fabrics along the corresponding seam lines using short stitches, approximately 18 to 20 stitches per inch. The tight stitches perforate the foundation paper so it can be torn away after the design is stitched.

Trace a foundation paper design onto lightweight paper, including the numbered sections of the design; draw a ½-inch border around all edges of the design. The tracing side of the foundation paper design will be faceup while the fabric pieces are sewn to the underside of the design. Use fabric pieces that measure approximately ¾ inch larger all around than the corresponding design sections.

Quilt Basics continued

Place and pin the first piece of fabric on the underside of the paper, right side up and extending at least ¼ inch beyond the first section. Trim seams after they are sewn. Having them extend more at this time ensures good design coverage. Hold the paper up to a light source to ensure the design is covered. Place and pin the fabric for the second section facedown on the first fabric at the adjoining seam line. Insert the foundation paper right side up under the sewing machine needle. Holding the fabric in place, and removing the pin if it is in the way, sew on the line between the first two sections, sewing a couple of stitches beyond the seam line.

Remove the paper and fabric from the machine, clip the threads, and turn the design to the fabric side. Open out the fabric and finger-press it. Trim excess seam allowance to a scant ¼ inch. Holding the foundation piece to a light source, place and pin the fabric for the third section. Sew on the seam line between the second and third sections. Finger press and trim the seam allowance. Continue sewing on pieces until the design is covered. Press the design from the fabric side. Carefully tear away the perforated paper. Use a rotary cutter and ruler to trim the seam allowance around the block to ¼ inch all around. Many of the blocks in this book can be adapted to paper piecing. Look for blocks and sections of blocks that have straight seams. Piece units; then sew the units together.

pieced block templates

All of the patterns in this book are finished-size to make creating templates easy and frustration-free. Use template plastic that is slightly frosted. You can see through it, spot it easily, and mark on it without smearing or smudging. For the blocks in this book avoid template plastic with printed grid, and avoid using cardboard for templates; it doesn't hold its shape with continuous use.

Using a ruler and fine-line permanent marker, trace block pieces onto the plastic. You'll add ¼-inch seam allowances when you cut out the pieces. (See information below for making appliqué templates.) Cut plastic on marked lines.

It is not necessary to move the template plastic when tracing each template. When several pieces are grouped together, draw them together, then cut them apart.

Note how the block patterns are labeled using letters. Use a permanent marking pen to label your templates with these same letters. The letters in each block are for that block only; piece B in one block isn't the same as B used in another block.

Instructions for making the blocks occasionally include the direction (4 times); this means to create the unit described a total of four times.

As you draw templates, note edges that will be on the outer edge of the block. Mark the template with an arrow along this edge to remind you to cut the fabric with arrow on the straight of grain, which helps prevent your block from stretching. Also mark which edges are to be sewn together.

To store blocks and templates, use small, clear zipper-type plastic bags to help keep items separate and easy to find. These easy-to-label bags are available at quilting and crafts stores as well as at the supermarket.

appliqué block templates

Trace the entire design onto template plastic as described above. Letter the design pieces on the template plastic. Cut out the template pieces.

Place templates faceup on the right side of fabric. Trace around the template. Make a dotted line on the template to indicate areas that will be covered by another shape.

transferring the pattern
from template to fabric

Lay out your fabric smoothly, wrong side up. Try to use fabric print elements to enhance the block design, centering a flower or stripe, for example. Position the template face down on the wrong side of the fabric.

For appliquéd blocks, mark fabric on the right side. Add the seam allowance (between ⅛ and ¼ inch) when you cut out each piece.

Trace around the template onto the fabric using a No. 2 pencil. This is the sewing line. Mechanical pencils are excellent, because they stay sharp. Don't choose one with lead that is too thin—the 0.7mm size is large enough. If using dark fabrics, choose light color leads.

For pieced blocks, use a ruler to add a ¼-inch seam allowance to all sides. You'll need a clear ruler printed with a fine-line ⅛-inch grid. Many rulers are not 100 percent accurate—the ¼-inch mark may be different from opposite sides of the ruler. If you own one of these, choose one edge and use only that edge.

You also can use the red ruler, which is exactly ¼-inch thick. This useful alternative to the clear ruler is about 1 inch thick, so it lifts your fingers, keeping them out of the way as you trace. Its bright red color makes it easy to spot on your sewing table.

Transfer the template marks, indicating which edges are to be sewn together for the seam allowances. This is especially helpful when, for example, a triangle has two sides with similar length.

prairie points

Prairie points are a fun way to add dimension to quilt blocks. To make prairie points, fold the square in half lengthwise with wrong sides together; press. With fold at top, fold and press each bottom corner up to the center, forming a triangle.

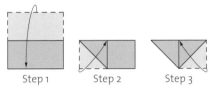

Step 1   Step 2   Step 3

yo-yos

Yo-yos add dimension and interest to flower centers. To determine the cutting size of the yo-yo circle, double the diameter of the finished yo-yo. Thus, for a 1-inch finished yo-yo, draw a 2-inch circle and add ⅛- to ¼-inch seam allowance.

To make several yo-yos the same size, make a plastic template. You can trace onto fabric once, make three or four layers of fabric, and cut several at one time. The sharper your scissors, the more layers you can cut.

To sew the yo-yos, thread quilting thread on a needle, and knot the end. Turn and stitch a ¼-inch seam.

Yo-yos are not the place for dainty stitches as they will put too many gathers in the circle and make the center hole too big.

Stitch very close to the edge of the fold to avoid a belly-button effect in the center of the completed yo-yo.

End sewing near the point where you began. Pull the thread firmly to draw the yo-yo closed. Secure with a few stitches.

Quilt Basics continued

mitered border corners

Pin a border strip to one edge of the quilt top, matching the center of the strip to the center of the quilt top edge. Sew together, beginning and ending the seam ¼ inch from the edge of the quilt top (see Diagram A, *below*). Allow excess border fabric to extend beyond each edge. Repeat with remaining border strips. Press the seam allowances toward the border strips.

Overlap the border strips at each corner (see Diagram B, *below*). Align the edge of the top border. With a pencil and triangle or ruler, draw along the edge of the triangle from the border seam to the outer corner. Place the bottom border on top and repeat marking process.

With right sides of adjacent border strips together, match the marked seam lines and pin (see Diagram C, *below*).

Beginning with a backstitch at the inside corner, stitch exactly on the marked lines to the outer edge of the borders. Check the right side of the corner to see that it lies flat. Trim excess fabric to leave a ¼-inch seam allowance. Press the seam open. Mark and sew each corner in this manner.

finished quilt sizes

Finished size is important in selecting a project and using or purchasing fabric. Finished quilt sizes can vary with the quilt design and fabric, personal choices, and bed style. For example, beds with solid, high footboards have no need for extra length at the foot of the bed and platform-style beds and four-poster beds require less width for drop than old-fashioned styles. Additional considerations include whether to combine the quilt with a dust ruffle or whether to provide length for a pillow tuck or use pillow shams.

Mattresses have standard length and width surface measurements, *below*. When measuring for a quilt, include the depth of the mattress and determine the length of drop to cover a box springs or side board, as well as the distance between the quilt and the floor.

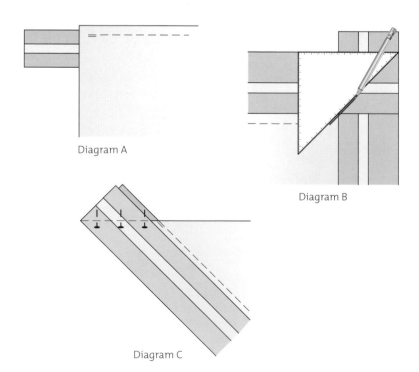

Diagram A

Diagram B

Diagram C

Standard mattress sizes:		Standard comforter sizes:	
Crib	27×52"	Twin	66×86"
Youth	33×66"	Full	76×86"
Twin	39×74"	Queen	86×88"
Full	54×74"	King	102×88"
Queen	60×80"		
King	78×80"		

Standard bedspread sizes:		Average dimensions for the four most popular quilt sizes:	
Twin	90×108"	Twin	67×87"
Full	96×108"	Full	82×97"
Queen	102×118"	Queen	88×103"
King	120×118"	King	106×103"

calculating sizes

To calculate finished size for a quilt, measure the surface dimension of the mattress. To these measurements add the following:

◆ 8 to 10 inches to the length for pillow tuck; eliminate this measurement if you plan to use pillow shams.

◆ the drop from the surface width of the mattress toward the floor, considering whether to cover a box springs or side board or to allow a dust ruffle to show.

◆ the drop from the foot of the bed to the floor, or the amount to tuck between the mattress and a footboard.

◆ 2 to 3 inches to the length and width measurements to allow for take-up by quilting.

figuring yardage for backing & binding

Unless wide fabric is used for backing the quilt, you will have to cut and piece together yardage. Use the following chart as a guide to figure the amount of yardage to purchase and how to piece the backing. Cut binding strips on the straight grain and seam together lengths for the total length needed. Fold the strip in half, wrong sides together, and press. Sew the raw edge of the binding strip to the raw edge of the layered quilt top using a 1/4-inch seam allowance, unless using heavier fabric than 100-percent woven cotton (such as flannel or heavy weaves). Using a walking foot to sew the binding to the quilted project helps to eliminate puckers.

Join the ends of the bias strips by folding or stitching them together. Turn the binding to the backing of the quilt and hand-sew the binding in place using blind hemstitching.

Bed size	Quilt size	Backing	2½-inch binding*
Twin and Full	67×87" 82×97"	5 yards; cut in half lengthwise, selvages removed. Seam together the lengths of the cut pieces with one full width of fabric.	¾ yard
Queen and King	88×103" 106×103"	8½ yards; cut fabric into three lengths, selvages removed. Seam together the three lengths.	⅞ yard

*cut across the width of the fabric (to finish ½ inch)

Index

Inspiring Quilt Designs

Quilt Block Patterns

Stitch Diagrams

Appliqué Stitch

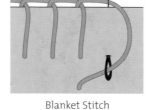

Blanket Stitch

Chain Stitch

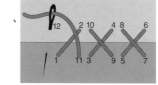

Cross-stitch

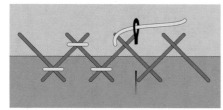

Featherstitch

French Knot

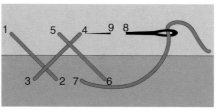

Herringbone

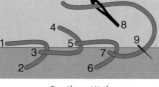

Herringbone with Couching

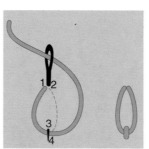

Lazy Daisy Stitch

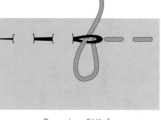

Running Stitch

Satin Stitch

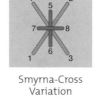

Smyrna-Cross Variation

Stem Stitch

Straight Stitch